How to Prepare For the CAT/6*

*CAT/6 is a registered trademark of Educational Testing Service, which was not involved in the production of and does not endorse this product

6th Grade Edition

By Todd Kissel
Dale Lundin
Nancy Samuels

CARNEY EDUCATIONAL SERVICES
Helping Students Help Themselves

Special thanks to Rim Namkoong, our illustrator

Copyright © 2005 by Carney Educational Services
All rights reserved. No part of this book may be reproduced or transmitted in any form or by any means, electronic or mechanical, including photo-copying and recording, or by any information storage or retrieval system.

This book is dedicated to:

The moms and dads who get up early and stay up late. You are the true heroes, saving our future, one precious child at a time.

All the kids who don't make the evening news. To the wide-eyed children, full of love, energy, and wonder. You are as close to perfection as this world will ever see.

TABLE OF CONTENTS

An Overview of the CAT/6 Test
Why did California change from the SAT 9 to the CAT/6   1
What does the CAT/6 seek to measure   1
Why do schools give standardized tests   2
What about criticism of standardized tests   2

How Your Child Can Improve His/Her Score On Standardized Tests
The importance of reading   3
The importance of building a larger vocabulary   3
The importance of following written directions   4
    Select the best answer   4
    Answer the easy questions first   5
    Eliminate any unreasonable answer choices   5
    Do math questions on paper when necessary   6

LANGUAGE ARTS
Word Recognition   7
Vocabulary and Concept Development   10
Structural Features of Informational Materials and Analysis of
    Grade-Level Text   20
Expository Critique   26
Spelling   35
Sentence Structure, Grammar, Punctuation, and Capitalization   46
Structural Features of Literature, Narrative Analysis of Grade-Level
    Text, and Literary Criticism   58
Answer Key   63

MATH
Computation Skills   65
Number Sense - fractions, decimals, and mixed numbers   73
Number Sense - fractions, ratios, proportions, and percentages   76
Number Sense - addition, subtraction, multiplication, and division of
    rational numbers   80
Algebra and Functions - verbal expressions   83

Algebra and Functions - algebraic expressions	85
Algebra and Functions - linear equations	86
Algebra and Functions - tables, graphs, and rules	89
Algebra and Functions - geometric patterns	91
Measurement and Geometry - plane, and solid shapes	93
Measurement and Geometry - two-dimensional figures	97
Measurement and Geometry - angles	100
Statistics, Data Analysis, and Probability - statistical measurement	103
Statistics, Data Analysis, and Probability - samples of a population	105
Statistics, Data Analysis, and Probability - theoretical and experimental	107
Mathematical Reasoning - decisions	111
Mathematical Reasoning - strategies	113
Answer Key	115

SOCIAL SCIENCE

Early Physical and Cultural Development of Mankind from the Paleolithic Era to the Agricultural Revolution	117
Early Civilizations of Mesopotamia, Egypt, and Kush	122
Early Civilizations of the Ancient Hebrews	127
Early Civilizations of the Ancient Greeks	130
Early Civilizations of India	136
Early Civilizations of China	139
The Development of the Roman Empire	142
Answer Key	148
Related Vocabulary	149

SCIENCE

Plate Tectonics and Earth's Structure	152
Shaping the Earth's Surface	155
Thermal Energy	157
Energy in the Earth System	159
Resources	163
Answer Key	164

An Overview of the CAT/6 Test

In the spring of 2002, the California Department of Education adopted the California Achievement Test, Sixth Edition (the CAT/6) as part of the state's Standardized Testing and Reporting System (STAR). The purpose behind this test is to provide California public school districts and parents with information about how their children are performing compared with other public school children from across the state. Keep in mind that this is a test of basic skills. It was written to assess the abilities of students only in specified areas of the curriculum. The CAT/6 is a standardized test, meaning that all public school children across California take the tests in the same manner and during the same months of the school year period. The directions given by teachers are the same, as are the amounts of time given to complete each testing section.

Why did California change from the SAT 9 to the CAT/6?

Over the last several years, the Stanford 9 (also referred to as SAT 9) standardized tests had generated controversy in some school districts due to errors in data analysis. Some of the important information reported by school districts was misused or analyzed incorrectly. These errors became quite costly to identify and correct. Additionally, some districts with large numbers of non-English speaking students encouraged parents to request waivers which would exclude their children from taking the SAT 9. Obviously, districts which sought to exclude such students from taking the test would receive higher scores than those districts which sought to test every student. In changing to the CAT/6, the California Board of Education decided to use a test with much more of a history in the state. The California Aptitude Tests were first developed in 1950, and are currently in use in nine other states. The CAT/6 will be administered by the Educational Testing Service (ETS), which is the largest testing firm in the nation.

What does the CAT/6 seek to measure?

Beginning in the spring of 2003, approximately 4.5 million students in grades 2-11 will be taking multiple choice tests in two main areas of the curriculum: Mathematics and Language Arts. The specific skills tested within Language Arts are vocabulary, reading comprehension, spelling, language mechanics (grammar), and language expression (word usage). The math sections of the test measure student mastery of math computation, math concepts and math applications. Students in grades 4-12 may be given a study skills subtest, which will measure how well student scan use information processing skills which they can use across all subject areas. The CAT test series also contains science and social studies subtests, but whether these will be used as part of the STAR program has yet to be determined.

Why do schools give standardized tests?

The CAT/6 gives schools an idea of how well they are teaching basic skills which all students need to be successful in the future. These skills are defined for schools in documents called "State Standards." The State Department of Education has spelled out for teachers, parents and students what they should be learning in each academic subject during a given school year. Schools receive data about how their students performed both individually and by grade level. Which state standards did students meet? Which standards need to be taught differently next year? How can schools help each child move toward meeting all the standards? All of these questions can be best answered by using the data provided by the CAT/6. Standardized tests are valuable because they are an objective way to measure how successfully schools are delivering the basics. The idea behind standardizing the test is this: if every public school student takes the same tests in the same way, then it is a fair way to compare schools and districts. If, for example, one school gave children an extra 5 hours to complete the test, then it would be an unfair advantage given to those children.

What about criticism of standardized tests?

In the last few years, criticism of standardized tests has mounted. Many parents and teachers say that preparing for these tests takes away time from valuable subjects like art, drama and music. They have also noted the stressful nature of these tests and question whether it is healthy to subject young children to this type of pressure to perform. Others believe these tests reward wealthy school districts in the suburbs, while they punish inner-city school districts with large numbers of non-English speaking students. While some of these criticisms are valid, they do not change the fact that standardized tests are widely regarded as the best way for schools to measure how they are teaching to the California State Standards. As long as the public asks public schools to prove they are doing an effective job educating children, these tests will be with us. The criticism of the Stanford 9 test resulted in replacing it with the CAT/6, which is ANOTHER standardized test.

As parents, we need to realize that these tests have become a fact of life in California public schools and help children prepare for them. Certainly, schools and teachers are primarily responsible for preparing your child for these tests. Yet parents have an important role to play. This book will give you many valuable tools you can use in helping your child do their best on this very important standardized test. It is the job of California public schools to teach to the standards, which are tested on the CAT/6, but your role as a reinforcer of skills and a supporter of your child's progress as a student cannot be ignored.

How Your Child Can Improve His/Her Score On ANY Multiple Choice Standardized Test

Your child has entered an educational world that is run by standardized tests. Students take the Scholastic Aptitude Test (SAT) to help them get into college and the Graduate Record Examination (GRE) to help them get into graduate school. Other exams like the ACT and the PSAT are not as well-known, but also very important to your child's future success. Schools spend a great deal of time teaching children the material they need to know to do well on these tests, but very little time teaching children HOW to take these tests. This is a gap that parents can easily fill. To begin with, you can look for opportunities to strengthen your child's reading and vocabulary skills as well as his/her ability to follow detailed written directions.

The importance of reading:

Students who do well on standardized tests tend to be excellent readers. They read frequently for pleasure and have a good understanding of what they have read. You can help support your child as a reader by helping him/her set aside a regular time to read each and every day. As you may know, children tend to be successful when they follow an established pattern of behavior. Even 15-20 minutes spent reading a magazine or newspaper before bedtime will help. Children should read both fiction and non-fiction material at home, as well as at school. Ask your child about what s/he has read. Help him/her to make connections between a book s/he is currently reading and a movie or a television show s/he has recently seen. THE BOTTOM LINE: Children who read well will do better on the test than children who do not. There is written material in all sections of the test that must be quickly comprehended. Even the math sections have written information contained in each question.

The importance of building a larger vocabulary:

As you may know, children who read well and who read often tend to have a large vocabulary. This is important since there is an entire section of the test that is devoted exclusively to the use of vocabulary words. You can support your child in attempting to improve his/her vocabulary by encouraging him/her to read challenging material on a regular basis. The newspaper is a good place to start. Studies have shown that many newspaper articles are written on a 4th to 5th grade reading level! Help your child to use new and more difficult words both in his/her own conversations and in his/her writings. If you use an advanced vocabulary when speaking to your children, don't be surprised if they begin to incorporate some of the new words into his/her daily speech. One of the most immediate ways to judge the intelligence of anyone is in his/her use of language. Children are aware of this too. THE BOTTOM LINE: Children who have an expansive vocabulary will do better on the test than children who do not. Find as many ways as possible to help build new words into your child's speech and writing.

The importance of following written directions:

The test is a teacher-directed test. Teachers tell students how to complete each section of the test and give them specific examples that are designed to help them understand what to do. However, teachers are not allowed to help students once each test has begun. The written script for teachers seems to repeat one phrase continually: "READ THE DIRECTIONS CAREFULLY." This is certainly not an accident. Students face a series of questions that cannot be answered correctly unless they clearly understand what is being asked. Help your child by giving him/her a series of tasks to complete at home in writing. Directions should be multi-step and should be as detailed as possible without frustrating your child. For example: "Please take out the trash cans this afternoon. Place all the bottles and cans in the blue recycling bin and place all the extra newspapers that are stacked in the garage in the yellow recycling bin." If children are able to follow these types of directions and are able to reread to clarify what is being asked, they will be at a tremendous advantage when it comes to the test.

THE BOTTOM LINE: Children who are able to follow a series of detailed, written directions will have a tremendous advantage over those who are unable to do so.

All of the previous suggestions are designed to be used before the test is actually given to help your child improve in some basic test-taking skills. Here are some strategies that you can teach your child to use once s/he is taking the test:

1. **SELECT THE BEST ANSWER.**

The test, like many multiple-choice tests, isn't designed for children to write their own answers to the questions. They will fill in a bubble by the four answer choices and select the BEST possible answer. Reading the question carefully is quite important, since the question may contain key words needed to select the correct answer. For example:

The first President of the United States was

a. John Adams.
b. James Madison.
c. George Washington.
d. Thomas Jefferson.

The correct answer is, of course, "c". Students would need to read the question carefully and focus on the key word in the question: "first". All of the names listed were Presidents of the United States early in our history, but only choice "c" contains the name of our first President. Looking for key words like "least" or "greater" will help your child to select the best answer from among the choices given.

2. ANSWER THE EASY QUESTIONS FIRST.

The test contains a series of timed tests. Children who waste time on a difficult question found at the beginning of a test may run out of time before they finish the entire test. A good strategy is to skip anything that seems too difficult to answer immediately. Once your children have answered every "easy" question in the section, they can go back through the test and spend more time working on the more time-consuming questions. If students are given only 30 minutes to answer 25 reading vocabulary questions, they shouldn't spend much more than a minute on each one. Wasting four or five minutes on one question is not a good idea, since it reduces the amount of time your child will have to work on the rest of the test. Once time runs out, that's it! Any questions left unanswered will be counted wrong when the test is machine scored. Working on the easier questions first will allow your child to make the best use of the allowed time.

3. ELIMINATE ANY UNREASONABLE ANSWER CHOICES.

No matter how intelligent your child is, it is inevitable that s/he will come to a test question that s/he finds too difficult to answer. In this situation, the best thing to do is to make an "educated guess." If students can eliminate one or more of the answer choices given, they have a much greater chance of answering the question correctly.

For example:

Select the word below that means the same as the underlined word:

Jennifer became enraged when she found out her diary had been read.

   a. mournful
   b. furious
   c. pleased
   d. depressed

Even if your child didn't know that "b" is the best answer choice, s/he could certainly eliminate choice "c" from consideration. Clearly, Jennifer would not be "pleased" to find out her diary had been read.

4. DO MATH QUESTIONS ON PAPER WHEN NECESSARY.

The math sections of the test cause children problems because several of the answer choices seem like they could be correct. The only way to select the best answer choice for some math questions is to do the math calculation on scratch paper. The answer choices given for these questions are written to discourage guessing.

For example:

Eileen has saved $3245 to buy a car. Her aunt gave her another $250 as a gift. How much does she have in all?

   a. $3595
   b. $4495
   c. $3495
   d. $3485

The correct answer is "c", but it is hard to select the correct answer because all of the answer choices seem similar. The best way to determine the correct answer would be to add $3245 and $250 on scratch paper.

> If you work with your children with these simple strategies, you will find that they will approach these tests with confidence, rather than with anxiety. Teach your children to prepare and then to approach the test with a positive attitude. They should be able to say to themselves, "I know this stuff, I'll do a great job today."

Carney Educational Services — How to Prepare for the CAT/6

LANGUAGE ARTS

Content Cluster: WORD RECOGNITION

Objective: To evaluate the student's knowledge of the meaning of grade-level-appropriate words.

> **Parent Tip:** Read, read, read! Read *with* your child. Read *to* your child. *Listen* to your child read. Those activities will provide a meaningful context in which to improve your child's reading, speaking, and writing vocabularies. Keep track of new words that he or she encounters during the reading section Make a point to try to use them in conversation and encourage your child to do so. The more your child hears them and pronounces them at home, the more willing he or she will be to use them in other contexts.
>
> The words that are presented in the exercises in this section are words that are likely to appear in sixth grade literary selections and history/social science texts. For additional vocabulary that is specific to the content of sixth grade social studies, refer to the word lists that appear at the end of the social science section of this book.

Select the answer that gives the best definition of the word given or the best synonym for it.

Example:

severe

a. thin
b. troubled
c. harsh
d. solemn

The correct answer is choice "c" because *harsh* is the word closest in meaning to the word *severe*. (Try the words in a phrase or sentence to test the choices: "He was worried that he would receive a *severe* punishment. He was worried that he would receive a *harsh* punishment." If you do not recognize a word, use the strategies described in the next content cluster, Vocabulary and Concept Development, to give you clues about the word's meaning.)

1. capable

   a. worthy
   b. able to do
   c. necessary
   d. smart

2. gratitude

   a. not needed
   b. amount given
   c. freedom
   d. being thankful

3. abolish
   a. do away with
   b. continue
   c. warn
   d. take prisoner

4. lawful
   a. not governed by rules
   b. stolen
   c. allowed by law
   d. confession

5. unlawful
   a. governed by rules
   b. stolen
   c. allowed by law
   d. not allowed by law

6. loyalty
   a. being truthful
   b. being hopeful
   c. being faithful
   d. being certain

7. majority
   a. smallest group
   b. greater part
   c. amount less than half
   d. wealthy

8. supreme
   a. weak
   b. only
   c. highest
   d. first

9. symbol
   a. something that stands for something else
   b. picture
   c. instrument
   d. surface

10. vow
    a. solemn
    b. promise
    c. sacrifice
    d. holy

11. disciple
    a. leader
    b. patrol
    c. follower
    d. director

12. fiction
    a. part of the whole
    b. historical event
    c. splinter group
    d. made-up story

13. voluntary
    a. done by choice
    b. done by accident
    c. done by force
    d. done with pay

14. accustomed
    a. frequent
    b. usual, used to
    c. acceptable
    d. accidental

15. annual

   a. angry
   b. part time
   c. yearly
   d. flowered

16. deceive

   a. receive
   b. promise
   c. lie
   d. practice

17. impudent

   a. important
   b. young and foolish
   c. rudely impolite
   d. very shy

18. migrate

   a. huge headache
   b. winter sleep
   c. misinterpret
   d. move to another place

19. descent

   a. lack of interest
   b. honorable
   c. coming down
   d. horrible

20. omit

   a. hide
   b. give out
   c. leave out
   d. change slightly

21. decrease

   a. to make less or become less
   b. disappear
   c. distract
   d. to become bigger

22. rebel

   a. one who resists authority
   b. one who fights for truth
   c. one who gets angry
   d. one who follows

23. hostile

   a. environment
   b. angry
   c. rumpled
   d. hilly

24. servitude

   a. treachery
   b. honesty
   c. quiet
   d. slavery

25. massive

   a. religious
   b. work of art
   c. huge
   d. not aggressive

Content Cluster: VOCABULARY AND CONCEPT DEVELOPMENT

Objectives: To evaluate the student's: (1) knowledge of word origins and word relationships; (2) understanding of figurative language and words with multiple meanings; (3) knowledge of frequently used foreign words in English; (4) understanding of "shades of meaning" in related words; and (5) skill in using word, sentence, and paragraph clues to determine the meaning of unknown words.

> **Parent Tip:** Help your child to become word conscious--to analyze words, to look for patterns among words, to be aware of the relationships among words, and to distinguish nuances of meaning among synonyms. As you analyze words, remember that roots, prefixes, and suffixes give clues to word meanings. Start analyzing words that your child knows and understands, then apply the process to unfamiliar words. Another useful strategy for finding the meaning of an unfamiliar word is to analyze the context in which a word is used in a sentence or paragraph.

Choose the best answer.

1. Which of the following is <u>not</u> considered figurative language?

    a. reader's theater
    b. a simile
    c. a metaphor
    d. personification

2. Which of the following sentences is a simile?

    a. He worked night and day to accomplish his dream to become a doctor.
    b. He had worked so hard that his hands were as tough as the bark of a sycamore tree.
    c. Few people admired his sour expression and bullish attitude.
    d. none of the above

3. Which of the following sentences is a metaphor?

    a. Her furry dog resembles a walking dish mop.
    b. Her dog is a walking dish mop.
    c. Her dog is as fluffy as a walking dish mop.
    d. none of the above

4. Personification is
   a. a type of character with a strong personality.
   b. a type of novel with comic characters.
   c. a type of metaphor in which a non-human thing is given human qualities.
   d. a type of tragic character with a flawed personality.

5. Which of the following sentences is an example of personification?
   a. After days of wandering through the wilderness, we were consumed with thoughts of a returning home to a warm bath.
   b. Her flowers were as wilted as a spinach salad.
   c. The newborn colt was as hungry as he was frisky.
   d. Before the lights went out, the clouds cried their tears and the thunder warned us to awaken our candles from their slumber.

Select the choice that makes sense in both sentences.

6. His subjects considered him to be a _____ ruler.
   Wait for me for _____ a moment.
   a. fair
   b. just
   c. powerful
   d. cruel

7. He considered his broken arm a _____ inconvenience.
   He could not legally sign the contract because he was a _____.
   a. military
   b. particular
   c. natural
   d. minor

8. We share your _____ regarding the potential danger _____ by the hole.
   If the artist's gallery becomes a growing _____, it will be because of the way he _____ the subjects in his photographs.
   a. concern, posed
   b. recommendation, caused
   c. position, caught
   d. thought, arranged

9. From the moment I opened the first page, I found the book very _____.
   I am having difficulty _____ the spill with this cloth.

   a. attaching
   b. constructing
   c. absorbing
   d. enlightening

10. I need to _____ this check before I go to the bank.
    I am not sure which candidate I will _____.

    a. support
    b. reject
    c. cash
    d. endorse

11. I am too weak to perform any _____ labor.
    If the car won't start, be sure to consult the _____.

    a. dictionary
    b. manual
    c. difficult
    d. company

Identify the root that tells the core meaning of each of the following words.

12. pedestrian

    a. walk
    b. destroy
    c. an
    d. ped

13. portable

    a. table
    b. ortab
    c. port
    d. able

14. magnify

    a. if
    b. y
    c. ic
    d. magnus

15. thermos

    a. her
    b. therm
    c. mos
    d. thermometer

16. activity

    a. al
    b. act
    c. ty
    d. y

17. anonymous

    a. onym
    b. tony
    c. mouse
    d. an

18. metropolis

   a. polis
   b. push
   c. slip
   d. met

19. description

   a. pit
   b. tion
   c. script
   d. de

Read the words in each exercise. Find their common root. Select the choice that contains the root and its meaning.

20. monarch, anarchy, oligarchy, matriarch, patriarch

   a. *on*, shape
   b. *arch*, ruler
   c. *ma*, machine
   d. *mon*, butterfly

21. telephone, phonics, megaphone, microphone, phonograph

   a. *eleph*, big
   b. *on*, on
   c. *noc*, notice
   d. *phon*, sound

22. nova, novelty, innovation, novice, renovate

   a. *nov*, new
   b. *ice*, cold
   c. *vow*, old
   d. *velt*, gold

Choose the best answer.

23. A prefix is
   a. part of a word that sounds like the way it is spelled.
   b. a letter or syllable added to the beginning of a root to change its meaning.
   c. a letter or syllable added to the end of a word that changes its meaning.
   d. a foreign word that is commonly used in English.

24. A suffix
   a. is part of a word that is added to the beginning of a root to change its meaning.
   b. is a part of a word that can stand alone and have meaning.
   c. is added to the end of a word to change its meaning or to change a word from one part of speech to another.
   d. changes a root to mean its opposite.

Read the words in each of the following exercises and select the choice that gives the meaning of the prefix or suffix.

25. preface, prevent, precede, predict, preview, prepaid, prepare

    a. paid
    b. before
    c. see
    d. say

26. counterattack, counterpart, counterclockwise, counterintuitive, counteract

    a. table
    b. against, in opposition to
    c. round
    d. again

27. nonsense, nonfiction, nonexistent, nonsense, nondescript

    a. know
    b. imaginary
    c. not
    d. only

28. dehydrate, decrease, decline, decentralize, depart

    a. down, the opposite of
    b. more, moving toward
    c. divide
    d. small

29. monotheistic, monopoly, monotone, monolith, monologue, monolingual

    a. monkey
    b. money
    c. one, alone
    d. mighty

30. faultless, powerless, clueless, priceless, speechless, heartless

    a. cruel
    b. power
    c. listen
    d. without

31. wisdom, kingdom, freedom, childhood, statehood, adulthood

   a. top
   b. state, condition of
   c. down
   d. thing

32. Buddhism, Judaism, Confucianism, capitalism, communism, socialism

   a. belief or doctrine
   b. fame
   c. study of
   d. ability to

33. biology, archaeology, physiology, anthropology, psychology

   a. mind
   b. school
   c. study of
   d. college

Select the English meaning of the following foreign words or words derived from other cultures. Select the best meaning for any underlined word.

34. The candidate studied until he discovered his opponent's <u>Achilles heel</u>.

   a. sore foot
   b. weak spot
   c. Greek myth
   d. quick sprint

35. The governor was interested in preserving the <u>status quo</u> for the time being.

   a. new arrangement
   b. fighting words
   c. mathematical equation
   d. the way things are

36. chaos

   a. shiny and bright
   b. chemical
   c. distant stars
   d. disorder and confusion

37. spartan

   a. tricky
   b. fighting
   c. simple, without luxury
   d. sharp

38. terra firma

   a. solid ground
   b. at sea
   c. trees on fire
   d. election day

Read the following paragraph and then select the meaning of the underlined words.

It had been a tough election. There had even been a [39] recount conducted after the election results had been announced. For weeks we had [40] burned the midnight oil studying the voters' responses to our survey. It seemed that the voters in the [41] precinct were in [42] accord on the issue of ethics in government, but remained divided on one critical issue, the [43] abolition of speed laws in the [44] vicinity of the rural area. Until the last ballots had been counted, it was [45] too close to call. Now, however, it was a time for a celebration. With genuine sincerity, the opposition had called campaign headquarters to [46] concede their loss and to congratulate our candidate on her victory. We thanked them for making what [47] undoubtedly had been a difficult phone call, then invited them to an [48] impromptu gathering to eat a snack and [49] reiterate our pledge to refrain from holding a grudge against them. They rushed to our offices only to find us snoring with our heads on our desks, exhausted from the [50] rigor of the campaign. Needless to say, we postponed the celebration.

39. a. poll
    b. telephone survey
    c. another counting
    d. questionnaire

40. a. started a fire
    b. questioned
    c. worked very late
    d. cooked dinner

41. a. district within boundaries
    b. perimeter
    c. outskirts of town
    d. precise

42. a. agreement
    b. disagreement
    c. disarray
    d. denial

43. a. requirement
    b. putting an end to
    c. addition
    d. effect

44. a. visiting area
    b. hallway
    c. background
    d. region nearby

45. a. time to telephone
    b. time to pray
    c. difficult to predict
    d. obvious

46. a. argue
    b. wonder about
    c. brag about
    d. admit

47. a. without a doubt
    b. with great doubt
    c. doubtful
    d. questionable

48. a. interfering
    b. deliberately slow
    c. late
    d. spur of the moment

49. a. recite
    b. wonder
    c. say again and again
    d. interpret again

50. a. rhythm
    b. severity
    c. fun
    d. timing

Choose the best answer.

51. Which word would be the most effective one to use regarding the destruction of an abstract concept such as a long-standing law or custom?

    a. destroy
    b. annihilate
    c. abolish
    d. reduce

52. Which of the following words implies potential power, or a natural aptitude to do something without necessarily having acquired the skill to do it?

    a. capacity
    b. ability
    c. will
    d. pride

53. Which of the following words implies that someone is impartial and not taking sides?

    a. uninvolved
    b. uninterested
    c. disinterested
    d. adversarial

54. Which of the following words refers to something that generally has a historical basis, but has become exaggerated throughout years of retelling?

    a. mythical
    b. fictional
    c. imaginary
    d. legendary

55. Which of the following words has the <u>most</u> negative connotation?

    a. firm
    b. resolute
    c. stubborn
    d. pigheaded

56. Which of the following words has the least negative connotation?

    a. arrogant
    b. proud
    c. conceited
    d. egotistical

57. Which of the following words connotes the least amount of emotion?

    a. annoyed
    b. furious
    c. irate
    d. enraged

58. Which of the following words connotes the most intense amount of activity?

    a. busy
    b. occupied
    c. hectic
    d. active

59. Which of the following words has the least negative connotation?

    a. uncommon
    b. bizarre
    c. peculiar
    d. weird

60. Which of the following words does not belong with the others?

    a. unpolluted
    b. pure
    c. pristine
    d. scrubbed

Content Cluster: STRUCTURAL FEATURES OF INFORMATIONAL MATERIALS AND ANALYSIS OF GRADE-LEVEL TEXT

Objectives: To evaluate the student's: (1) knowledge of the features and organizational patterns of resources such as textbooks and popular media; (2) skill in summarizing and outlining information to clarify meaning; (3) ability to follow multiple-step instructions for preparing applications; and (4) skill in clarifying main ideas by identifying their relationships to other sources and related topics.

> **Parent Tip:** The skills tested in this content cluster improve with familiarity and practice. Encourage your child to be an "active" reader—one who makes predictions and judgments about the material's content. Active readers of informational materials make it a practice to quickly scan a piece to note its component parts and look for subtitles that will give them clues about what they will read. They look at the pictures, too. They make mental or written notes about what they think they will read. Then, as they read the piece in its entirety, they watch to see whether their predictions are confirmed or invalidated. They pause at various points in their reading to make sure they can restate in a simple way what they have read.

Choose the best answer.

1. A reader who wants to read different people's opinions about current events is likely to find them in the _____ section of the newspaper.

    a. front page
    b. headline
    c. editorial or "op-ed"
    d. sports

2. Which of the following features are you likely to find in an on-line newspaper that you would not find in a traditional newspaper?

    a. archived or older stories
    b. links to other resources
    c. expanded comics
    d. a and b only

3. Which of the following is <u>not</u> an important feature in works of non-fiction?

    a. table of contents
    b. index
    c. glossary
    d. biography

4. Which of the following choices is an example of a compare-and-contrast organizational pattern?

   a. My brother and I are the only ones in our math classes who can solve complicated problems in our heads.
   b. My brother is very quiet and shy until he feels comfortable around you.
   c. Although both of my siblings love music, my brother enjoys listening to classical music in the morning, while my sister prefers waking up to a rock beat.
   d. If I compare two items in price, I may need to use subtraction skills.

5. When writing a paper that discusses the timing of a series of events, which organization pattern would you probably want to use?

   a. compare-and-contrast
   b. chronological order
   c. stream of consciousness narrative
   d. inferences and abstract examples

6. When writing a paper that discusses the attitudes of two Roman emperors about slavery, which organizational pattern would you probably want to use?

   a. compare-and-contrast
   b. personal style
   c. chronological order
   d. stream of consciousness

7. If you are trying to explain something in writing that is very complicated, which organizational pattern would you probably want to use?

   a. compare and contrast with something that the reader probably already understands
   b. stream of consciousness narrative
   c. alternating flashbacks with future events
   d. inferences and abstract examples

8. When taking notes about things you read or hear,

   a. it is important to always use complete sentences.
   b. you do not need to pay attention to the main idea and supporting details.
   c. never draw pictures to help you remember things.
   d. none of the above

9. When researching a report using many sources,
   a. it is not important to keep track of which source you are summarizing.
   b. take notes in your own words unless the exact words are especially interesting.
   c. it is important to copy every detail you read.
   d. it is not helpful to organize with an outline before you write a first draft.

Read the application and answer the questions about it that follow.

FRIENDS of the ART MUSEUM & GARDENS
APPLICATION for MEMBERSHIP

1. NAME _____
2. SOCIAL SECURITY #(optional) _____
ADDRESS:
3. STREET _____
4. CITY _____
5. STATE ____ 6. ZIP _____
7. DATE OF BIRTH _____ 8. AGE ____
TYPE OF MEMBERSHIP:

	YEARLY FEE	LIFE FEE
9. INDIVIDUAL ADULT	☐ $15	☐ $50
10. CHILD (UNDER 12 YRS.)	☐ $5	
11. STUDENT	☐ $10	
(ALL AGES WITH STUDENT ID)		
12. FAMILY	☐ $50	☐ $200
(INCLUDES 2 ADULTS, 3 CHILDREN, 2 SENIORS)		
13. SENIOR (OVER 60 YRS.)	$10	☐ $35
14. SCHOOL	☐ $50	
(FREE ENTRY FOR 4 CLASSES)		

If applying for student membership, complete lines 15, 16, and 22. For school membership, complete lines 15-21. All other applicants skip to line 22. ALL APPLICANTS COMPLETE LINE 23.

15. SCHOOL NAME _____
16. SCHOOL ADDRESS _____
17. FIELD TRIP COORDINATOR'S NAME _____
18. SCHOOL PHONE _____
19. SCHOOL FAX _____
20. SCHOOL E-MAIL ADDRESS _____
21. SIGNATURE OF SCHOOL PRINCIPAL _____
22. SIGNAURE OF PARENT (IF UNDER 18) _____
23. SIGNATURE OF APPLICANT _____

THIS APPLICATION, ACCOMPANIED BY THE APPROPRIATE MEMBERSHIP FEE, ENTITLES THE APPLICANT(S) TO:
  A. FREE MUSEUM ENTRY ON ALL VISITS
  B. PRIORITY TICKETS TO SPECIAL EVENTS & EXHIBITS
  C. FREE PARKING
  D. 10% DISCOUNT IN THE MUSEUM GIFT SHOP

YEARLY MEMBERSHIPS ARE VALID FOR ONE YEAR FROM THE DATE OF THIS APPLICATION.

10. Regarding line #2 on the application,

    a. everyone must write a social security number on the form.
    b. only adults must write their social security number on the form.
    c. the applicant may choose whether or not to provide his or her social security number on the form.
    d. membership requires that the application have a social security card.

11. Mrs. Smith is a teacher who is responsible for completing the application for her school's membership. How much money will that membership cost and who must sign the application?

    a. $15; the school principal
    b. $50; the museum director and the school field trip coordinator
    c. $50; the school principal, the school field trip coordinator, and Mrs. Smith
    d. $50; the school principal and Mrs. Smith

12. John is a nine-year-old fourth grade student. What membership option will cost him the least amount of money this year and what signatures will be required?

    a. Student membership; John and his parent
    b. Child membership; John and his parent
    c. Child membership; John
    d. Child membership; John and his field trip coordinator

13. If John's great-grandmother applies for a family membership, which of the following lines must she complete on the application?

    a. 15 and 16
    b. 21 and 22
    c. 21
    d. 23

Read the selection and choose the best answers to the questions that follow.

Henry David Thoreau was an American naturalist, writer and philosopher who lived from 1817 to 1862. In 1845, Thoreau built a cabin at Walden Pond, near Concord, Massachusetts. He lived there for 2 years, 2 months, and 2 days. During his stay at the pond he tried to simplify his life and live with the barest essentials. He wanted to free himself from slavery to material things. He worked his small plot of land, visited with friends, recorded his observations of nature, and wrote many essays.

During those famous two years, Thoreau spent one night in jail. As an act of protest, he refused to pay his yearly poll tax. This non-violent act was Thoreau's way of stating his opposition to our Mexican War. As he explained in his 1849 essay entitled "Civil Disobedience," "Under a government which imprisons any unjustly, the true place for a just man is also a prison."

Thoreau was not only seeking his personal emancipation from slavery to materialism. In "Civil Disobedience," Thoreau expressed his disdain for a government that would allow slavery of any kind. He wrote:

> The proper place to-day [for the state's freer spirits]
> is in her prisons. It is there that the fugitive slave,
> and the Mexican prisoner on parole, and the Indian
> come to plead the wrongs of his race, should find them,
> on that separate but more free and honorable ground—
> …the only house in a slave-state in which a free man
> can abide with honor.

Thoreau's legacy of non-violent civil disobedience—disobeying unjust laws in order to achieve justice—has endured more than a century into modern times. It influenced Mahatma Gandhi in his attempt to win India's right to self-rule, and it was revived again by Martin Luther King, Jr. as a rationale for Americans to disobey the segregation laws of the American South in the 1960's.

14. A good title for this selection is

   a. The Roots of the Fight for Self-Rule in India
   b. Henry David Thoreau, a Naturalist
   c. Simplify, Simplify
   d. The Birth of Civil Disobedience

15. In an outline of this passage, which of the following would not be included in a section entitled "Two years at Walden Pond?"

   a. Thoreau tried to simplify his life.
   b. Thoreau foresaw the death of slavery in America.
   c. Thoreau spent a night in jail as a protest.
   d. Thoreau believed in non-violent disobedience to unjust laws.

16. The quoted passages from Thoreau's essay could also be used to illustrate

   a. his belief in the religious aspects of Transcendentalism.
   b. his friendship with Ralph Waldo Emerson.
   c. his support of the abolitionist movement.
   d. his belief that the government which governs least, governs best.

Content Cluster: EXPOSITORY CRITIQUE

Objectives: To determine whether the student is able to: (1) analyze the sufficiency of evidence that an author offers in support of a conclusion; (2) make reasonable assertions about a text; and (3) identify instances of unsupported inferences, fallacious reasoning, persuasion, and propaganda in text.

> **Parent Tip:** Expository writing serves to explain an idea or process. Help your child to be a thoughtful consumer of the spoken and written word. Talk with him or her about the difference between fact and opinion, and objective and persuasive language. You might start by analyzing infomercials and current event talk shows. What is the purpose of the show? Look for underlying assumptions that may not be explicitly stated. Try to identify the biases of the speakers. It is this kind of analysis that will serve your child well in critiquing expository writing.

Read the selection and choose the best answers to the questions that follow.

Henry David Thoreau was an American naturalist, writer and philosopher who lived from 1817 to 1864. He was a good friend of Ralph Waldo Emerson, another American poet, essayist, and philosopher who challenged traditional thought. Thoreau and Emerson belonged to an influential literary circle in Concord, Massachusetts, and they edited *The Dial*, a magazine devoted to Transcendentalism. Another member of the club was Bronson Alcott. His daughter, Louisa May Alcott, wrote the beloved American novels, *Little Women* and *Little Men*.

The Transcendentalists were as much a part of a philosophic movement as a literary one. Reacting against the ever-increasing influence of science, the Transcendentalists argued that people should rely on intuition to understand reality. They believed in the "divine sufficiency of the individual," that is, that within each individual lay the key to nature, history and, ultimately, the universe. Emerson expressed his beliefs in his first book, *Nature*, in 1836. Transcendentalists viewed nature as a living mystery, but a mystery that could be understood. To study oneself was to study nature.

In keeping with the Transcendentalist motto, "know thyself," in 1845, Thoreau borrowed a plot of land from Emerson, and built a cabin at Walden Pond, near Concord. He lived there for 2 years, 2 months, and 2 days. During his stay at the pond he tried to simplify his life and live with the barest essentials. He wanted to free himself from slavery to material things. He worked his small plot of land, visited and entertained friends, recorded his observations of nature, and wrote many essays. Living the Transcendentalist philosophy, he sought to know and become one with the world. Thoreau's eloquent plea for people to simplify life so that its meaning may become clearer, is recorded in his now famous book, *Walden, or Life In the Woods*, in which he wrote, "I frequently tramped eight or ten miles through the deepest snow to keep an appointment with a beech tree, or a yellow birch, or an old acquaintance among the pines. I once had a sparrow alight upon my shoulder for a moment while I was hoeing in a

village garden, and I felt that I was more distinguished by the circumstance than I should have been by an epaulet I could have worn."

During his lifetime, in addition to seeking his own personal emancipation from slavery to material things, Thoreau worked tirelessly with other members of his family to abolish all forms of slavery. He personally helped runaway slaves escape to Canada. In his 1849 essay, "Civil Disobedience," Thoreau expressed his disdain for a government that would allow slavery of any kind. He wrote:

> The proper place to-day [for the state's freer spirits]
> is in her prisons. It is there that the fugitive slave,
> and the Mexican prisoner on parole, and the Indian
> come to plead the wrongs of his race, should find them,
> on that separate but more free and honorable ground—
> ...the only house in a slave-state in which a free man
> can abide with honor.

Thoreau was an outspoken voice in the woods; a nonconformist who questioned America's passion for material possessions, business, and success. He spoke out against economic injustice and slavery. He believed in self-reflection and unity with nature. He was a man who put his principles into action.

1. A good title for this selection is

   a. Emerson and Nature
   b. The Birth of Civil Disobedience
   c. The Influence of Transcendentalism on Thoreau
   d. The Evil of Slavery

2. Which of the following conclusions is supported by adequate evidence in this passage?

   a. Thoreau questioned the definition of success in America.
   b. Thoreau spoke out against economic injustice.
   c. Thoreau was a man who put his principles into action.
   d. Thoreau did not understand science.

3. After reading this passage, it is reasonable to assert that

   a. Thoreau used his dissatisfaction to support anarchy.
   b. Thoreau was a hermit who hated people.
   c. Thoreau routinely practiced civil disobedience.
   d. Thoreau was a nature lover.

4. Which line from the passage best supports the proposition that Thoreau was not a hermit?

   a. "Thoreau was an outspoken voice in the woods..."
   b. "He worked his small plot of land, visited and entertained friends, recorded his observations of nature, and wrote many essays."
   c. He believed in self-reflection and unity with nature.
   d. During his stay at the pond he tried to simplify his life and live with the barest essentials.

5. Which line from the passage best supports the proposition that Thoreau was a nature lover?

   a. "I frequently tramped eight or ten miles through the deepest snow to keep an appointment with a beech tree, or a yellow birch, or an old acquaintance among the pines. I once had a sparrow alight upon my shoulder..."
   b. "Thoreau was an outspoken voice in the woods;"
   c. "He worked his small plot of land, visited with friends, recorded his observations of nature, and wrote many essays."
   d. "To study oneself was to study nature."

6. Which of the following choices is an <u>unstated</u>, underlying assumption of this passage?

   a. America had become increasingly materialistic by the 1840's.
   b. Americans in the North helped runaway slaves to escape.
   c. Thoreau had friends who were Transcendentalist writers.
   d. The Transcendentalists were part of a philosophic and literary movement.

7. In the first paragraph of the passage, which of the following sentences could be deleted without destroying any meaning?

   a. Henry David Thoreau was an American naturalist, writer and philosopher who lived from 1817 to 1864.
   b. He was a good friend of Ralph Waldo Emerson, another American poet, essayist, and philosopher who challenged traditional thought.
   c. Thoreau and Emerson belonged to an influential literary circle in Concord, Massachusetts, and they edited *The Dial*, a magazine devoted to Transcendentalism.
   d. Another member of the club was Bronson Alcott. His daughter, Louisa May Alcott, wrote the beloved American novels, *Little Women* and *Little Men*.

8. Which of the following conclusions is supported by appropriate and sufficient evidence in this passage?

    a. "That government is best which governs least."
    b. Thoreau was the father of civil disobedience.
    c. "The mass of men lead lives of quiet desperation."
    d. Thoreau tried living out the principles of Transcendentalism.

9. From the information given in the passage, it would be false reasoning to assert that

    a. Louisa May Alcott was a Transcendentalist.
    b. Emerson, Thoreau, and Bronson Alcott were Transcendentalists.
    c. other members of Thoreau's family were abolitionists.
    d. Transcendentalists were interested in philosophy and the nature of the world.

10. From the information given in the passage, it would be reasonable to assume that

    a. the author of the passage did not respect Thoreau.
    b. Thoreau avoided making controversial statements.
    c. *The Dial* was a source of propaganda of the Transcendentalists.
    d. Thoreau was not an introspective person who enjoyed nature.

Content Cluster: WRITING STRATEGIES AND WRITING APPLICATIONS

Objectives: To evaluate the student's knowledge of: (1) the stages of the writing process; (2) how to write for a specific audience and purpose; (3) how to write narrative, expository, persuasive, and descriptive texts; and (4) research, organizational, and drafting strategies.

> **Parent Tip:** The California Standard is for sixth grade students to be able to write narrative, expository, persuasive, and descriptive texts of 500 to 700 words. A good way to help them meet that standard is to show them examples of what they are trying to achieve. Have your child read many examples of high quality writing in each genre. Analyze the form of each selection, in effect, creating an outline that shows the structure or skeleton of the piece. Examine well-written paragraphs to see how the author deals with only one topic in each one. Identify the ways that the author makes his thoughts easy to follow. Finally, make sure your child expresses himself in writing every day in some way. It may be a diary or journal; it may be a poem or a plot outline for a short story; or it may be a summary of a story heard on a news broadcast. Writing skills are improved like every other skill in life—through regular, informed, purposeful practice.

The questions in this section relate to the various paragraphs. Read each paragraph and choose the best answer to the questions.

I have always loved horses and ponies—equines of all shapes, colors, and sizes. Ever since I read Marguerite Henry's *Misty of Chincoteague*, however, the Chincoteague ponies have held a special place in my heart. The legends and facts that surround the real-life Chincoteague ponies are fascinating.

1. In writing the body of this piece, the next paragraphs should discuss

    a. other titles of Marguerite Henry's novels.
    b. different breeds of horses and ponies.
    c. the legends and facts relating to the Chincoteague ponies.
    d. horses throughout the ages.

2. Which of the following sentences would make an appropriate topic sentence for the next paragraph?

    a. The Chincoteague ponies are thriving today.
    b. There are many legends that explain how wild horses of Spanish origin came to live on a tiny island off Virginia.
    c. After two fires destroyed the Town of Chincoteague in the 1920's a small group of men organized a volunteer fire company.
    d. *Misty of Chincoteague* was Marguerite Henry's second book.

Use the following paragraph to answer questions 3 – 12.

[1] Another legend tells how Spanish pirates purposely set the ponies' ancestors on the shores of Chincoteague. [2] The heavily-laden galleon was carrying horses that escaped from the cargo hold and swam to safety on nearby Chincoteague's shore. [3] One widely accepted legend tells how a 16th Century Spanish galleon on its way to South America was shipwrecked on the shoals of Assateague Island during a violent storm. [4] How the wild breed came to live at Chincoteague is a mystery. [5] It maintains that in the 17th Century, mainland farmers who wanted to avoid fencing requirements and paying livestock tariffs turned the ponies' ancestors out there to graze. [6] However they reached the island, they flourished throughout the centuries to become the hardy breed that they are today. [7] Finally, The U.S. National Park Service's story is the least exciting but is considered by many to be the most plausible explanation.

3. This paragraph is lacking

    a. unity, because all the sentences do not relate to the same idea.
    b. adequate detail to clearly explain the ideas presented.
    c. coherence, because the thoughts do no follow a logical order.
    d. examples or facts to help develop the topic sentence

4. In order to make the meaning of this paragraph clearer, it would help the writer to

    a. find the topic sentence and put it first.
    b. look for sentences that support or clarify the topic sentence.
    c. look for connecting words and contrasting words to make decisions about sentence order.
    d. all of the above

5. The topic sentence of this paragraph is

    a. [4] How the wild breed came to live at Chincoteague is a mystery.
    b. [1] Another legend tells how Spanish pirates purposely set the ponies' ancestors on the shores of Chincoteague.
    c. [6] However they reached the island, they flourished throughout the centuries to become the hardy breed that they are today.
    d. [3] One widely accepted legend tells how a 16th Century Spanish galleon on its way to South America was shipwrecked on the shoals of Assateague Island during a violent storm.

6. A good conclusion for this paragraph is

   a. [4] How the wild breed came to live at Chincoteague is a mystery.
   b. [1] Another legend tells how Spanish pirates purposely set the ponies' ancestors on the shores of Chincoteague.
   c. [6] However they reached the island, they flourished throughout the centuries to become the hardy breed that they are today.
   d. [3] One widely accepted legend tells how a 16th Century Spanish galleon on its way to South America was shipwrecked on the shoals of Assateague Island during a violent storm.

7. In determining a logical sentence order for this paragraph, you can guess that

   a. sentence [1] probably does not come before sentence [3] because the word "another" is a transitional word.
   b. sentences [1] and [2] probably do not go together because the words "purposely" and "escaped" imply different scenarios.
   c. sentences [2] and [3] probably go together because they both use the word "galleon," and the words "heavily-laden," "escaped," "shipwrecked," "storm," and "violent storm" explain one event.
   d. all of the above

8. The sentence order that would logically develop this paragraph is

   a. 4, 3, 2, 1, 7, 5, 6
   b. 1, 2, 6, 7, 3, 4, 5
   c. 7, 6, 5, 4, 3, 2, 1
   d. none of the above

9. Which of the following sentences is <u>not</u> an example of a supporting detail in this paragraph?

   a. [4] How the wild breed came to live at Chincoteague is a mystery.
   b. [2] The heavily-laden galleon was carrying horses that escaped from the cargo hold and swam to safety on nearby Chincoteague's shore.
   c. [5] It maintains that in the 17th Century, mainland farmers who wanted to avoid fencing requirements and paying livestock tariffs turned the ponies' ancestors out there to graze.
   d. none of the above

10. When revising this paragraph, which of the following organizational patterns would probably be the least effective approach?

   a. chronological order
   b. spatial order
   c. order of importance or reader interest
   d. comparison and contrast

11. Which of the following sentences would be the strongest transition between the two paragraphs?

   a. How the wild breed came to live at Chincoteague is a mystery.
   b. There are many legends that explain how wild horses of Spanish origin came to live on a tiny island off Virginia.
   c. However they reached the island, they flourished throughout the centuries to become the hardy breed that they are today.
   d. The heavily-laden galleon was carrying horses that escaped from the cargo hold and swam to safety on nearby Chincoteague's shore.

12. If you wanted to plan a vacation on Chincoteague Island, which would be the least effective way to get information?

   a. write a letter to the Chincoteague Island Chamber of Commerce
   b. conduct an internet search regarding Chincoteague Island
   c. go to the library to conduct a search of articles in travel magazines or travel sections of various newspapers
   d. write a letter to the editor of your local newspaper to request information

13. You enter a contest in which you must write an essay about your favorite book and how it has influenced your life. Your essay should include

   a. descriptive language.
   b. quotes from the book that support why you like it.
   c. the reasons why you like the book and how it has affected your life.
   d. all of the above

14. A good way to store addresses in a computer would be in

   a. e-mail
   b. a search engine
   c. a database
   d. a modem

15. What is the appropriate page orientation for a chart that is wider than it is long?

    a. landscape
    b. portrait
    c. column
    d. tabular

16. Which of the following research topics is narrow enough in scope to be thoroughly covered in 700 words?

    a. horse breeds throughout history
    b. the wild ponies of Assateague and Chincoteague Islands
    c. dog breeds of the world throughout history
    d. the cultures and wars of Ancient Greece and Rome

17. Which of the following is not necessary to cite in a bibliography?

    a. the books you read in preparation for writing your paper
    b. the books you quoted in your paper
    c. information from the internet
    d. your original thoughts

18. Which of the following should be included in a thoughtful written response to literature?

    a. an insightful interpretation of the work
    b. facts, details, examples, and explanations from a variety of sources
    c. examples from the text that support your ideas and interpretations
    d. all of the above

19. Which of the following is not an appropriate element of a persuasive composition?

    a. stating your position clearly in favor of, or against, the proposition
    b. anticipating and addressing counter-arguments and reader concerns
    c. making personal attacks on the opponents
    d. supporting your position with well-organized and relevant information

Content Cluster: SPELLING

Objective: To evaluate the student's spelling skills.

> **Parent Tip**: A child will have an easier time spelling words that he or she has read and written frequently in context. The good news is that in a language of over one million words, we use the same few thousand words repeatedly. Encourage your child to read rich literature. With respect to writing, when he or she consistently misspells a word, encourage him or her to print the word carefully and keep it for future reference with other personal spelling demons. It will help to say and touch each letter to commit the sequence of the letters to memory. Keep the personal spelling demon list handy during homework time.

Fill in the blank with the correctly spelled word.

1. A triangle has three sides and three _____.

    a. angles
    b. angels
    c. angells
    d. angeles

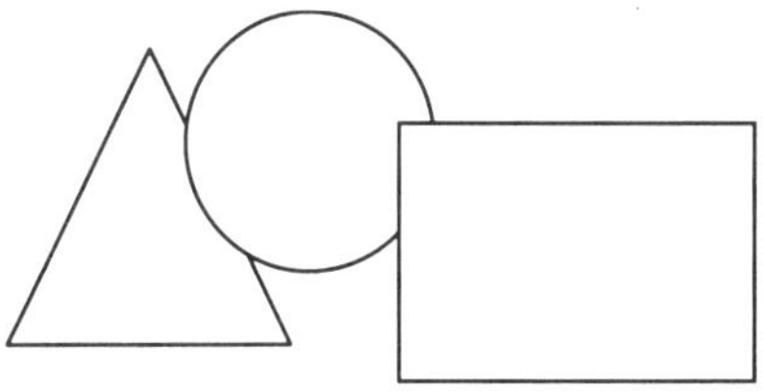

2. He was absolutely _____ he knew the answer.

    a. curtain
    b. certain
    c. certian
    d. certan

3. As she wandered through the crowd, she was _____ to find her mother.

    a. disparate
    b. desperate
    c. desprate
    d. desparat

4. He found the magician's ability to fool people quite _____.

    a. fassinating
    b. facinating
    c. facinnating
    d. fascinating

5. He was the _____ person in line to buy a ticket.

   a. fourty-fourth
   b. fourty-forth
   c. forty-fourth
   d. forty forth

6. When they reached the beach, they jumped in the water _____.

   a. immediately
   b. imediatly
   c. imedeitly
   d. immedeitly

7. Yesterday we _____ our horses to the meadow to graze.

   a. lead
   b. led
   c. ledd
   d. laed

8. I am not sure _____ book he wants to read.

   a. wich
   b. witch
   c. whitch
   d. which

9. They changed _____ _____ after they fell in the mud.

   a. they're close
   b. there clothes
   c. their clothes
   d. their cloes

10. _____ _____ all the people going?

    a. Were where
    b. Ware were
    c. Wear were
    d. Where were

11. Several _____ decided to enter the woodworking contest at the fair.

    a. wommen
    b. women
    c. woman
    d. wiminn

12. Don't wait _____ you are too tired to exercise.

    a. until
    b. untill
    c. til
    d. till

13. I hope I studied _____ to do well on the math test.

    a. enuf
    b. enuff
    c. enouph
    d. enough

14. Our teacher is _____ ready to give us a reward.

    a. all most
    b. allmost
    c. almost
    d. almoste

15. Never run _____ a street.

    a. accross
    b. accros
    c. acrost
    d. across

16. I hope _____ time to eat lunch.

    a. its
    b. it's
    c. its's
    d. its'

17. The cookie was so good I could have eaten the _____ box.

   a. whole
   b. hole
   c. wholle
   d. holy

18. _____ _____ the teacher thought the joke was funny.

   a. Evryone eccept
   b. Every one accept
   c. Everywon ecsept
   d. Everyone except

19. The time _____ slowly because I had nothing to read while I was waiting.

   a. pased
   b. passed
   c. past
   d. passt

20. During the _____ month I have been able to exercise more often.

   a. pased
   b. passed
   c. past
   d. passt

21. We _____ in the _____ of equal rights for all.

   a. believe, principle
   b. beleive, prinscipl
   c. belief, prinsipul
   d. believe, principal

22. Mrs. Taylor is the _____ of our school.

   a. principle
   b. prinscipl
   c. prinsipul
   d. principal

23. Their _____ crop was wheat.

   a. principle
   b. prinscipl
   c. prinsipul
   d. principal

24. He had to pay interest on the _____ of the loan.

   a. principle
   b. prinscipl
   c. prinsipul
   d. principal

25. Sara is younger _____ her sister.

   a. thin
   b. than
   c. then
   d. thun

26. If _____ not coming to our house, can we go over _____?

   a. there, their
   b. their, there
   c. they're, there
   d. their, they're

27. The _____ of us were _____ tired _____ do any more work.

   a. to, two, too
   b. too, to, two
   c. two, too, to
   d. two, to, to

28. I can't decide _____ I like rainy _____.

   a. whether, weather
   b. weather, whether
   c. wether, whether
   d. weather, weather

29. I _____ tell the truth.

   a. all ways
   b. allways
   c. al ways
   d. always

30. Every student should know his or her _____.

   a. address
   b. adres
   c. adress
   d. addres

31. With every _____ the athlete's _____ became more determined.

   a. atempt, atitude
   b. attempt, attitude
   c. attepmt, attatude
   d. atempt, attatude

32. As we _____ through the _____, all we could think about was _____.

   a. traveld, dezert, dezirt
   b. travelled, dessert, desert
   c. traveled, desert, dessert
   d. traveled, dessert, dessert

33. Houdini was an _____ _____ artist.

   a. eccellent, excape
   b. eccelent, iscape
   c. excellent, escape
   d. excillint, ecscape

34. How could we _____ our _____ of direction so quickly?

   a. lose, sense
   b. lose, sence
   c. loose, cents
   d. loose, sence

35. My brother and I now have _____ rooms.

   a. seprate
   b. seperate
   c. sapperite
   d. separate

36. I _____ hope his _____ is _____ to the audience.

   a. sincerly, speach, intresting
   b. sincerely, speech, interesting
   c. sinsereley, speech, intersting
   d. sincearly, speach, interessting

37. _____ at the door?

   a. Whose
   b. Whos'
   c. Who's
   d. Whose'

38. I know _____ shoes these are.

   a. whose
   b. whos'
   c. who's
   d. whose'

39. Make sure _____ taking _____ books home to study.

   a. you're, you're
   b. you're, your
   c. your, your
   d. you're, you're

40. I _____ the stick away, _____ my friend _____ we should play with it.

   a. through, though, thought
   b. threw, thought, throughout
   c. threw, though, thought
   d. through, tho, throat

41. We hear a story about a man who once _____ _____ eggs for breakfast.

   a. eight, ate
   b. ate, eight
   c. ate, ate
   d. eight, eight

42. We were _____ shocked at the noise level when the band _____ playing and the crowd was _____.

   a. quiiet, quitt, quite
   b. quiet, quite, quit
   c. quit, quiet, quite
   d. quite, quit, quiet

Choose the correctly spelled plurals and verb forms.

43. box, sock

   a. boxes, boxed, socks, socked
   b. boxs, boxd, sockses, socced
   c. boxxes, boxt, socks, sockt
   d. boxes, boxxed, sockes, socket

44. body, toy

   a. bodys, tois
   b. bodys, toyes
   c. bodies, toys
   d. boddies, toys

45. bench, push

   a. benches, bencht, pushs, pushd
   b. benches, benched, pushes, pushed
   c. benchs, benchd, pushs, pushd
   d. benchs, benchet, pushes, pusht

46. country, half

   a. countrys, halfs, halfed
   b. countries, halves, halved
   c. countries, halfs, haved
   d. countrys, halves, halved

47. target, promise

   a. targets, targeted, promises, promised
   b. targgetts, targgetted, promise, promised
   c. targetts, targetted, promisses, promissed
   d. targets, targetted, promises, promisst

48. permit, set

   a. permitts, permitted, setts, setted
   b. permmits, permmited, sets, sett
   c. permits, permited, sets, setted
   d. permits, permitted, sets, set

Identify the word that is spelled incorrectly.

49. against	accross	address	accept
50. eighth	acsident	acceptable	apologize
51. auther	argument	almost	among
52. all right	analies	always	article
53. apology	apologize	awfull	athlete
54. believe	bibliography	become	beginer
55. achieve	busness	bargain	attitude
56. beautiful	because	benefitted	beauty
57. catagory	conscience	conscientious	cruise
58. choice	critic	criticism	colledge
59. decision	discribe	disapprove	disappear
60. disappoint	diffrence	curious	desperate
61. curiousity	curiosity	divided	doesn't
62. embarass	embarrass	entirely	excellent
63. fascinating	fasinating	forest	foreign

	a	b	c	d
64.	guest	disgusted	discusted	definitely
65.	definitly	extremely	exaggerate	environment
66.	excape	escape	finally	describe
67.	experience	except	guest	gest
68.	happened	doctor	disease	happenned

Identify the word that is spelled correctly.

	a	b	c	d
69.	hapiness	extraordinary	endevor	enimy
70.	friend	familier	friendlyness	furnicher
71.	goverment	genious	governer	height
72.	imediatly	immediatly	immediately	emergancy
73.	instint	instant	imaginery	influensed
74.	intelligint	interested	interupt	intrested
75.	isnt	expirt	judgment	judgement
76.	lonliness	lonliness	lonelyness	loneliness
77.	ocur	ocurr	occur	occurr
78.	usually	usully	usuly	usualy
79.	mointain	mountin	mountan	mountain
80.	mistery	mystery	mystiry	mysteryous
81.	notisible	noticable	noticeable	notiseable
82.	oposite	opposite	oppisit	oppasit
83.	picture	practise	prejadice	persanal
84.	puting	quizes	realise	piece
85.	posibal	possible	possable	posible

	a	b	c	d
86.	receive	recieve	receve	receave
87.	remembir	restraunt	restaurant	replys
88.	referring	refering	seperate	sevral
89.	sinse	similar	similir	simalir
90.	tommorrow	tomorow	tomorrow	resourses

Content Cluster: SENTENCE STRUCTURE, GRAMMAR, PUNCTUATION, AND CAPITALIZATION

Objectives: To evaluate the student's knowledge of: (1) the use of simple, compound, complex, and compound-complex sentences to effectively express complete thoughts; (2) subject-verb agreement with compound subjects; (3) indefinite pronouns; (4) present perfect, past perfect, and future perfect verb tenses; and (5) the use of colons, semicolons, and commas; and (6) correct capitalization.

Parent Tip: Your child's mastery of the skills emphasized in this section will help him or her develop a clear, effective writing style. Once the content of a piece of writing is fully developed, a writer must pay close attention to the standard English conventions in order to turn a rough draft into a final, polished piece of writing.

The exercises in this section contain bold-faced text, followed by a series of questions that refer to that text. Read the sentences typed in bold, and then choose the best answer to the questions that follow them.

[1] **The distinguished but verbose former Senator from Virginia spoke eloquently for hours about the issue of big government in America.** [2] **Many of the listeners rose to their feet and cheered wildly at the end of his speech.**
[3] **The less attentive people in the audience were awakened by the applause.**
[4] **What an embarrassment was that!**

1. Sentence [1] is a

    a. run-on sentence.
    b. compound sentence.
    c. compound-complex sentence.
    d. simple sentence.

2. The complete subject of sentence [1] is

    a. senator.
    b. a senator from Virginia.
    c. a senator from Virginia spoke eloquently.
    d. The distinguished but verbose Senator from Virginia.

3. The simple subject of sentence [2] is

   a. listeners.
   b. many listeners.
   c. many.
   d. many of the listeners.

4. The simple and complete subject of sentence [4] is

   a. what.
   b. embarrassment.
   c. an embarrassment.
   d. that.

5. The compound predicate of sentence [2] is

   a. rose.
   b. cheered.
   c. rose, cheered.
   d. rose to their feet and cheered wildly at the end of his speech.

[5] As many of the listeners rose to their feet and cheered wildly at the end of his speech, the less attentive people in the audience were awakened by the applause.

6. The sentence structure of sentence [5] is

   a. simple
   b. complex
   c. compound
   d. compound-complex

7. The structure of sentence [5] is

   a. a dependent or subordinate clause followed by an independent clause.
   b. an independent clause followed by a dependent clause.
   c. two dependent clauses.
   d. two independent clauses

8. The comma in sentence [5]

   a. is necessary.
   b. is unnecessary.
   c. should be replaced by a semicolon.
   d. should be replaced by a colon.

9. If the order of the phrases in sentence [5] is switched, the comma

    a. is necessary.
    b. is unnecessary.
    c. should be replaced by a semicolon.
    d. should be replaced by a colon.

10. If the first word of sentence [5] is omitted and a conjunction is added after the comma, the new sentence

    a. makes no sense.
    b. becomes a compound-complex sentence.
    c. becomes a complex sentence.
    d. becomes a compound sentence.

11. If the first word of sentence [5] is omitted and no conjunction is added,

    a. the comma should remain in the new sentence.
    b. the comma should be replaced with a colon
    c. the comma should be replaced with a semicolon
    d. no punctuation is needed between the two clauses.

12. If the only change made to sentence [5] is to replace the comma with a period, the words "As many of the listeners rose to their feet and cheered wildly at the end of his speech"

    a. become a complete sentence.
    b. become a simple sentence.
    c. become a sentence fragment.
    d. becomes an independent phrase.

13. Whenever the words *and, or, but, nor, for, so,* or *yet* join two independent clauses,

    a. they follow a comma.
    b. they follow a semicolon.
    c. they follow a period.
    d. no punctuation is necessary.

14. Which of the following choices is a compound-complex sentence?

    a. I have never ridden on the Ferris wheel, but I scream every time I ride the roller coaster.
    b. Although I have visited the amusement park several times, I have never ridden on the Ferris wheel, but I have screamed my way through the roller coaster's loop-the-loops on many occasions.
    c. Although I have visited the amusement park several times, I have never ridden on the Ferris wheel. I have, however, screamed my way through the roller coaster's loop-the-loops on many occasions.
    d. All of the above

In each of the following exercises, decide whether the text is without error, or whether it should be revised according to one of the choices.

15. My dad and I struck a deal, he bought the groceries and I made the dinner.

    a. no errors
    b. I and my dad struck a deal. He bought the groceries and I made the dinner.
    c. My dad and I struck a deal; he bought the groceries, and I made the dinner.
    d. My dad and me struck a deal; He bought the groceries; I made the dinner.

16. Our teacher told us we were to noisy and so we quieted down imediately.

    a. no errors
    b. When our teacher told us we were to noisy, we quited down immediately.
    c. When our teacher told us we were too noisy, we quieted down immediately.
    d. Our teacher told us we were too noisy, because we quieted down immediately.

17. I want to buy a new book to read, however I need to wait for my allowance.

    a. no errors
    b. I want to buy a new book to read; however, I need to wait for my allowance.
    c. I want to buy a new book to read. However, I need to wait for my allowance.
    d. both choice *b* and choice *c* are correct

18. I liked the novel. Mostly it was funny. And always interesting; although sad in parts.

    a. no errors
    b. Although the novel was sad it was interesting, and I liked it because it was mostly funny.
    c. The novel. I liked it, because it was always sad and funny and interesting.
    d. Although the novel was sad in parts, I liked it because it was mostly funny, and always interesting.

19. Everybody in our family works around the house and we all get an allowance that we're earning. We divided the chores, I rake leaves, my sister sorts the laundry, and my brother takes out the garbage. So it's all pretty fair anyway most of the time.

   a. no errors
   b. In our family, the children earn an allowance by helping around the house, and the chores are divided fairly evenly. I rake leaves; my sister sorts the laundry; my brother takes out the garbage.
   c. I rake leaves and my sister sorts the laundry in our family and my brother takes out the garbage. So we all divide the chores and do our work. It's fair that way.
   d. In our family, the children earn an allowance by helping around the house. I am dividing the chores evenly so that I raked the leaves, my sister is sorting the laundry and my brother will take out the garbage.

The questions in this section refer to the bold-faced. Choose the best answer to the questions.

[6] 1234 Writing Lane
     Mistakesville, CA 90000
     January 1, 2000

[7] Chincoteague island chamber of commerce
    P.O. Box 1
    Chincoteague Island, VA 23336

[8] **Dear sir or madam,**

[9] I'm interested in visiting the island this summer to see the pony auction. [10] I have never visited virginia before, could you please send me the following information. [11] ASAP-- I need to know when it is and places to stay and can my Dad rent a car anywhere. [12] Sending a map is important! [13] Is there other fun things to do around where you are?
[14] **And by the way: Do the ponies cost alot.** [15] You can send all the stuff I need to me right away, ok? [16] Because I can't wait, I'm looking forward to it so much.

[17] **Love,**

[18] **Linda Lacksgrammar**

20. The inside address of this letter

   a. is section [6], and it indicates that this is a friendly letter.
   b. is section [7], and it indicates that this is a friendly letter.
   c. is section [7], and it should be revised to capitalize the words *island, chamber,* and *commerce.*
   d. is section [8], and it indicates that this is a business letter.

21. The salutation of this letter

    a. is section [7], and it contains no errors.
    b. is section [7], and it should be revised to capitalize the words *island, chamber,* and *commerce*.
    c. is section [8], and it contains no errors.
    d. is section [8], and it should be revised to capitalize the words *sir* and *madam*, and end with a colon.

22. The complimentary close of this letter

    a. should be changed to *Sincerely, Yours truly*, or *Respectfully yours*.
    b. is appropriate for a business letter.
    c. is section [18] and should be handwritten, not typed.
    d. is section [17] and requires no change.

In each of the following exercises, decide whether the text is without error, or whether it should be revised according to one of the choices.

23. Section [8]

    a. no errors
    b. Dear Sir or Madam;
    c. Dear Sir or Madam,
    d. Dear Sir or Madam:

24. [9] I'm interested in visiting the island this summer to see the pony auction.

    a. no errors
    b. I am interested in visiting Chincoteague Island this summer to see the pony auction.
    c. I am interested in visiting the island of chincoteague to see the pony auction this summer.
    d. I'm interested in visiting the Island this Summer to see the Pony Auction.

25. [10] I have never visited virginia before, could you please send me the following information. [11] ASAP—I need to know when it is and places to stay and can my Dad rent a car anywhere. [12] Sending a map is important! [13] Is there other fun things to do around where you are?

   a. no errors
   b. I have never visited Virginia before. Could you please send me the following information as soon as possible? I need to know when it is, and places to stay, and can my dad rent a car anywhere? Sending a map is important! Are there other fun things to do around where you are?
   c. As soon as possible, please send me the following information: the auction date; hotel, motel, or apartment accommodations in the area; and places to rent a car. Because I have never visited Virginia before, I would also appreciate it if you could send me a map of the area and information about other points of interest in the vicinity.
   d. As soon as possible, please send me the following information; the auction date, hotel, motel, or apartment accommodations in the area, and places to rent a car. Because I have never visited Virginia before I would also appreciate it if you could send me a map of the area and information about other points of interest in the vicinity.

26. [14] And by the way: Do the ponies cost alot.

   a. no errors
   b. should be revised to read "And by the way, do the ponies cost a lot?" and should remain after sentence [13] in the body of the letter.
   c. should be revised to read "And, by the way, are the ponies expensive." and should be moved to follow sentence [9] in the body of the letter.
   d. should be included in a revision to sentence [11] that might read "As soon as possible, please send me the following information: the auction date; expected prices of ponies at the auction; hotel, motel, or apartment accommodations in the area; and places to rent a car."

27. [15] You can send all the stuff I need to me right away, ok? [16] Because I can't wait, I'm looking forward to it so much.

   a. no errors
   b. should be revised to read "Please send all the information I need to me right away. Because I can't wait; I'm looking forward to it so much." and should remain after sentence [14] in the same paragraph.
   c. should be revised to read "Please send the information to me at the address that appears above. I eagerly await your reply." and should start a new paragraph after sentence [14].
   d. should be revised to read "Sending all the information I need to me right away is important, okay? I can't wait; because I'm looking forward to it so much." and should start a new paragraph after sentence [14].

28. If one of the computers at school break; the teacher has a manual with instructions that come with it.

   a. no errors
   b. If one of the computers at school is broke, the teacher has a manual with instructions that come with it.
   c. If one of the computers at school breaks, the teacher has a manual with instructions that comes with it.
   d. If one of the computers at school are broken, the teacher has a manual with instructions that come with it.

29. Did the Police Officer say who would be talking to we boys about the problem.

   a. no errors
   b. Did the police officer say who would be talking to us boys about the problem?
   c. Did the Police Officer say who would be talking to us boys about the problem?
   d. Did the police officer say whom would be talking to we boys about the problem?

30. Did your mother say to whom we would be speaking at the station?

   a. no errors
   b. Did your Mother say to whom we would be speaking at the Station?
   c. Did your mother say to who we would be speaking at the station?
   d. Did your Mother say to who we would be speaking at the Station?

31. "Didn't I warn you not to cross the street to chase a ball," mother cried angrily?

   a. no errors
   b. "Didn't I warn you not to cross the Street to chase a ball," Mother cried angrily?
   c. "Didn't I warn you not to cross the Street to chase a ball," mother cried angrily?
   d. "Didn't I warn you not to cross the street to chase a ball?" Mother cried angrily.

32. My favorite restaurant serves french food with a japanese influence but their table linens are imported from Italy.

   a. no errors
   b. My favorite Restaurant serves French Food with a Japanese influence, but their table Linens are imported from Italy.
   c. My favorite restaurant serves French food with a Japanese influence; but it's table linens are imported from Italy.
   d. My favorite restaurant serves French food with a Japanese influence, but its table linens are imported from Italy.

33. When she reads "Tom Sawyer" she thought about how long it would take her to paint the fence earning some extra money.

    a. no errors
    b. When she read <u>Tom Sawyer</u>, she thought about how long it would take her to paint the fence to earn some extra money.
    c. When she read "Tom Sawyer," she thinks about how long it's gonna take her to paint the fence to earn some extra money.
    d. When she read Tom Sawyer, she is thinking about how long it will take her to be painting the fence when she earned some extra money.

34. My Grandmother said that I'm not suppose to walk to the Market unless my friends' can come with me.

    a. no errors
    b. My Grandmother said that "I'm not suppose to walk to the Market," unless my friends can come with me.
    c. My grandmother said that I'm not supposed to walk to the market unless my friends can come with me.
    d. My grandmother said that I'm not suppose to walk to the market unless my friends can come with me.

35. The horses will have ridden in the trailer for four days before reaching the West Coast.

    a. no errors
    b. The horses will have rode in the trailer for four days since they left the west coast.
    c. The horses have rode in the trailer for four days since they left the West Coast.
    d. The horses have ridden in the trailer for four days before reaching the west coast.

36. The pedestrian could of seen the car coming toward him, if he only would of looked North before they crossed the street.

    a. no errors
    b. The pedestrian could have seen the car coming toward him if he only would have looked north before he crossed the street.
    c. The pedestrian could of seen the car coming toward him, if he only would of looked North before he crossed the Street.
    d. The pedestrian could have seen the car coming toward him, if he only would have looked North before having been acrossed the street.

37. Someday I hope to attend the University of California at Los Angeles to study drama, music, and literature, although I intend to take Biology 101 while I am there.

    a. no errors
    b. Someday I hope to attend the University Of California At Los Angeles to study Drama, Music, and Literature, although I intend to take Biology 101 well I'm there.
    c. Someday I hope to attend the university of California at Los Angeles to study drama, music, and literature. Although I intend to take biology 101 while I am their.
    d. Someday I hope to attend the University of California at Los Angeles to study drama, music, and literature; although I intend to take biology 101 while I am they're.

Choose the best answer.

38. Which words are <u>not</u> indefinite pronouns?

    a. I, you, he, she, it, we, they, them
    b. anybody, anyone, each, neither, nobody, one
    c. somebody, someone, no one, either, none
    d. both, few, many, several, all, any, most, some

39. Which sentence is <u>not</u> correct?

    a. One of the calculators is damaged.
    b. One of the calculators are damaged.
    c. The principal and her teachers want us to read more books.
    d. The principal, along with her teachers, wants us to read more books.

40. Which sentence is <u>not</u> correct?

    a. Here's the books with the beautiful illustrations.
    b. Here's the book with the beautiful illustrations.
    c. Here are the books with the beautiful illustrations.
    d. Here are the beautiful illustrations from the book.

41. Which sentence is <u>not</u> correct?

    a. Half of the cookies were gone.
    b. Half of the cookie was gone.
    c. Half of the cookies was gone.
    d. Half a cookie is better than none.

42. Which sentence is not correct?

    a. Everyone wants to know who the winner is.
    b. Each of the boys wants to know who the winner is.
    c. Either of the students are going to be the winner.
    d. Neither of the students is going to be the winner.

43. Which pronouns are always singular and always require a singular verb?

    a. many, several, everybody
    b. few, both, someone
    c. all, some, any, most, none
    d. either, neither, no one, someone, each, anybody

44. Which pronouns can be either singular or plural, depending upon the words that follow them?

    a. each, anyone, everybody, everyone, one
    b. few, both, many, several
    c. all, some, any, most, none
    d. either, neither, no one, someone, each, anybody

45. Which sentence is not correct?

    a. All of the baseball game was spent arguing with the umpire.
    b. All of the pieces of cake were eaten before we left home.
    c. None of the fruit was spoiled when we left the market.
    d. Some of the glasses of orange juice was spoiled.

46. Which sentence is not correct?

    a. Neither the teacher nor the students brought his work to class.
    b. Neither the student nor the teachers brought their papers to class.
    c. Neither the students nor the teacher brought his book to class.
    d. Neither the teacher nor the student brought her book to class.

47. Identify the sentence written in the present perfect tense.

    a. I write in my journal every day.
    b. I wrote in my journal every day.
    c. I have written in my journal every day.
    d. I shall write in my journal every day.

48. Identify the sentence written in the past perfect tense.

    a. She enjoyed her vacation because she went hiking every day.
    b. She had enjoyed her vacation because she had looked forward to it for so long.
    c. She will be enjoying her vacation because she loves the beach.
    d. She enjoys her vacation as she swims along the shore.

49. Identify the sentence written in the future perfect tense.

    a. They will practice playing the piano in preparation for the recital.
    b. They practice playing the piano every day in preparation for the recital.
    c. They are practicing the piano in preparation for the recital.
    d. They will have practiced playing the piano for hours by the time of the recital.

50. Which sentence is the least ambiguous?

    a. As she spoke to her favorite movie star, she was very embarrassed.
    b. As Jane spoke to her favorite movie star, she was embarrassed.
    c. As Jane spoke to Sherry Lane, her favorite actress, she was embarrassed.
    d. Jane was embarrassed as she spoke to her favorite movie star.

51. Which sentence is the least ambiguous?

    a. Several classmates thanked my mom for the cookies she baked for us as she waited in front of the school.
    b. As she waited in front of the school, several of my classmates thanked my mom for the cookies she baked for us.
    c. He watched the dogs sitting next to the door.
    d. Many people heard the noise outside the house.

Content Cluster: STRUCTURAL FEATURES OF LITERATURE, NARRATIVE ANALYSIS OF GRADE-LEVEL TEXT, AND LITERARY CRITICISM

Objectives: To evaluate the student's: (1) knowledge of the forms of fiction and their major characteristics; (2) analysis of character, plot, setting, theme, and point of view in literature; (3) analysis of the effects of symbolism, imagery, and figurative language in fictional and non-fictional texts; (4) knowledge of the features of poetry; and (5) skill in distinguishing between contrived or realistic plot, as in fact and fantasy.

> **Parent Tip:** Different forms of writing require a different level of engagement on the part of the reader. Much of poetry and prose can be read for the sheer enjoyment of the experience. When analysis is required, however, encourage your child to make judgments about the veracity and plausibility of what is written. Help him or her to examine the qualities of the characters and analyze the effect that the setting has on the plot. Discuss the theme that resonates in the work. Do the conflict and the theme ring true? Is there a message that can be applied in everyday life?

Choose the best answer.

1. Writing can be divided into two main categories,

    a. poetry and prose.
    b. edited and revised.
    c. interesting and figurative.
    d. imaginary and narrative.

2. Poetry is

    a. a kind of rhythmic writing
    b. uses imagery, similes, metaphors, and personification to try to appeal to the emotion and imagination of the reader.
    c. a form of writing that may or may not have a regular pattern of rhythm or rhyme.
    d. all of the above

3. A stanza is

    a. a random thought that does not fit into a theme.
    b. to a poem what a paragraph is to prose.
    c. a line in a rhyming poem.
    d. the attitude expressed by the poet.

4. Poetry written to sound like regular conversation is called

   a. talking verse.
   b. non-rhyming poetry.
   c. free verse
   d. no beat, no meter, no matter

5. In this stanza of Robert Frost's "Stopping By Woods On a Snowy Evening," what is the rhyme scheme?

   Whose woods these are I think I know
   His house is in the village though;
   He will not see me stopping here
   To watch his woods fill up with snow.

   a. 1 2 3 4
   b. A B C D
   c. A B B A
   d. A A B A

6. Meter can be described as

   a. the beat of the poem.
   b. the pattern of how the voice rises and falls in a poem.
   c. the pattern of accented and unaccented syllables in line of a poem.
   d. all of the above

7. "Stopping By Woods On a Snowy Evening" is written in

   a. iambic meter.
   b. iambic pentameter.
   c. with five meter feet.
   d. onomatopoeia.

8. "Stopping By Woods On a Snowy Evening" is written in

   a. internal rhyme
   b. end rhyme
   c. random rhyme
   d. initial rhyme

9. Oscar Wilde's line "Each narrow cell in which we dwell" is an example of

   a. internal rhyme.
   b. end rhyme.
   c. random rhyme.
   d. initial rhyme.

10. Prose can be divided into two main categories,

    a. poetry and free verse.
    b. sonnets and quatrains.
    c. fiction and non-fiction.
    d. biography and autobiography.

11. Which of the following are forms of fiction?

    a. bibliographies
    b. novels and short stories
    c. autobiographies
    d. newspaper science reports

12. Which of the following are key elements of fiction?

    a. plot, character, speed, oral tradition
    b. theme, plot, character, pace
    c. theme, plot, character, setting, point of view
    d. contrast, irony, psychological analysis

13. Which of the following elements is not usually part of the story's plot?

    a. an introduction to the characters and their conflict
    b. the climax, or most exciting moment in the story
    c. the resolution, or when the characters' problems may be solved
    d. the personification, when the reader begins to identify with a character

14. Characterization is the way that a writer reveals the personality of a character. Which of the following choices is not characterization?

    a. His room always looked like a cyclone had hit it and he routinely ignored his mother's request to pick up the dirty clothes strewn on the floor.
    b. The wind howled through the trees to wake Susan from her deep sleep.
    c. "I wish I could have a horse of my own to ride. I would work so hard to pay for it. I'd do anything. I would get up extra early to feed it before school. I would clean the whole barn and muck all the stalls twice a day. I'd do anything, Dad."
    d. As she heard the teacher call her to come to her desk, she felt her eyes fill with tears. She wondered if she would reach the desk before the dam broke.

15. Which of the choices in the preceding question contains a metaphor, a simile, or personification?

    a. none of the choices
    b. all of the choices
    c. choices a, b, and c
    d. choices a, b, and d

16. The point of view in a fictional work

    a. has nothing to do with the person who tells the story.
    b. has nothing to do with the way the story is told.
    c. can be determined by analyzing who tells the story.
    d. is the same as the setting and plot.

17. Which of the following is an example of the omniscient point of view?

    a. As the detective wove in and out of the shadows he wondered if the messenger had seen him. He worried that someone would discover his plan. Little did he know that the messenger was preoccupied looking for an address.
    b. I knew at once I could not hide the truth. It never works for me anyway. My face always tells the story.
    c. I saw the detective weave in and out of the shadows. What was he thinking? I would never know.
    d. I saw the detective weave in and out of the shadows. I could tell that he was following someone by the way he was hiding in the shadows.

The questions in this section refer to the following plot outline. Choose the best answer to the quesitons.

Jake Holden, age fourteen, describes his life as a pioneer in 1840's America. His story begins on the Natchez Trace and follows his travels with his parents and younger sister over the course of their adventure. During his journey west, he encounters people his own age who are establishing homesteads on their own. He imagines himself starting his own farm. He is torn between his feelings of family loyalty and his desire to prove that he is mature enough to make it on his own.

18. An example of a character's internal conflict in this story might be

    a. when an intruder enters the Holden's camp and steals their food.
    b. when Jake's horse becomes lame on the trail.
    c. when Jake is embarrassed that he is not starting out on his own.
    d. hunger and the search for food during the journey.

19. An example of external conflict in this story might be

    a. when Jake wonders how his family would get along without his help if he set out on his own.
    b. Jake's attempt to protect his sister from being teased in town.
    c. the family's struggle with feelings of regret for having left the comforts of home.
    d. Jake's sister's desire to believe in the predictions of a traveling fortune teller.

20. If Jake is a character with the qualities of moral courage and family loyalty, how might that affect the plot of the story and the resolution of Jake's inner conflict?

    a. Jake probably would yield to peer pressure.
    b. Jake probably would abandon his family and stake his own claim.
    c. Jake probably would help his family reach their destination before starting on his own.
    d. Jake probably would strike off on his own because of his resentment of his family.

21. Part of the story reads: "I reckon I won't be leavin' y'all. I couldn't bear to think of how y'all would be in a pickle without me to fix the broken wagon when it gets stuck in the mud." Pa just looked up and smiled. Ma promised me I'd never be sorry. Deep down, I believed she was right.

    a. The story is written in third-person point of view
    b. The story is written in dialogue narration form.
    c. The story is written in third-person omniscient point of view.
    d. The story is written in first-person point of view.

22. In the story, Jake and his sister meet a fortuneteller along the trail. She reads their fortunes.

    a. She is a minor character and can be disregarded.
    b. Only the family members mentioned in the first part of the story are relevant.
    c. Her presence in the story is likely to serve a literary purpose such as symbolizing Jake's concern about his future.
    d. She would not symbolize anything because symbolism is mainly found in poetry.

23. A possible theme for this story might be

    a. Your family's love for you is something to cherish.
    b. Hardship and travel go had in hand.
    c. Always listen to fortunetellers.
    d. Don't leave home.

LANGUAGE ARTS ANSWER KEY

Word Recognition
1. b
2. d
3. a
4. c
5. d
6. c
7. b
8. c
9. a
10. b
11. c
12. d
13. a
14. b
15. c
16. c
17. c
18. d
19. c
20. c
21. a
22. a
23. b
24. d
25. c

Vocabulary
1. a
2. b
3. b
4. c
5. d
6. b
7. d
8. a
9. c
10. d
11. b
12. d
13. c
14. d
15. b
16. b
17. a
18. a
19. c
20. b
21. d
22. a
23. b
24. c
25. b
26. b
27. c
28. a
29. c
30. d
31. b
32. a
33. c
34. b
35. d
36. d
37. c
38. a
39. c
40. c
41. a
42. a
43. b
44. d
45. c
46. d
47. a
48. d
49. c
50. b
51. c
52. a
53. c
54. d
55. d
56. b
57. a
58. c
59. a
60. d

Informational Materials
1. c
2. d
3. d
4. c
5. b
6. a
7. a
8. d
9. b
10. c
11. d
12. b
13. d
14. d
15. b
16. c

Expository Critique
1. c
2. c
3. d
4. b
5. a
6. a
7. d
8. d
9. a
10. c

Writing Strategies & Applications
1. c
2. b
3. c
4. d
5. a
6. c
7. d
8. a
9. a
10. b
11. b
12. d
13. d
14. c
15. a
16. b
17. d
18. d
19. c

Spelling
1. a
2. b
3. b
4. d
5. c
6. a
7. b
8. d
9. c
10. d
11. b
12. a
13. d
14. c
15. d
16. b
17. a
18. d
19. b
20. c
21. a
22. d
23. d
24. d
25. b
26. c

Carney Educational Services | How to Prepare for the CAT/6

27. c	64. c	5. c	42. c
28. a	65. a	6. b	43. d
29. d	66. a	7. a	44. c
30. a	67. d	8. a	45. d
31. b	68. d	9. b	46. a
32. c	69. b	10. d	47. c
33. c	70. a	11. c	48. b
34. a	71. d	12. c	49. d
35. d	72. c	13. a	50. d
36. b	73. b	14. b	51. b
37. c	74. b	15. c	
38. a	75. c	16. c	**Reading**
39. b	76. d	17. d	1. a
40. c	77. c	18. d	2. d
41. b	78. a	19. b	3. b
42. d	79. d	20. c	4. c
43. a	80. b	21. d	5. d
44. c	81. c	22. a	6. d
45. b	82. b	23. d	7. a
46. b	83. a	24. b	8. b
47. a	84. d	25. c	9. a
48. d	85. b	26. d	10. c
49. b	86. a	27. c	11. b
50. b	87. c	28. c	12. c
51. a	88. a	29. b	13. d
52. b	89. b	30. a	14. b
53. c	90. c	31. d	15. d
54. d		32. d	16. c
55. b	**Sentence**	33. b	17. a
56. c	**Structure,**	34. c	18. c
57. a	**Grammar,**	35. a	19. b
58. d	**Punctuation &**	36. b	20. c
59. b	**Capitalization**	37. a	21. d
60. b	1. d	38. a	22. c
61. a	2. d	39. b	23. a
62. a	3. c	40. a	
63. b	4. d	41. c	

6th Grade Edition   64

MATH

Content Cluster: COMPUTATION SKILLS

Objective: Students will have mastered the four arithmetic operations with positive and negative numbers, whole numbers, fractions, and decimals.

> **Parent Tip**: Students should have mastered the four operations with whole numbers, but it is important to revisit these skills. Make sure they **READ** the operation signs.

Whole Numbers -

Addition:

1. 87
    + 43
    a. 120
    b. 130
    c. 44
    d. 45

2. 139
    + 64
    a. 193
    b. 203
    c. 75
    d. 295

3. 647
    + 354
    a. 901
    b. 991
    c. 1,001
    d. 293

4. 122
    + 367
    a. 245
    b. 490
    c. 389
    d. 489

5. 9718 + 388 =
    a. 9,106
    b. 10,106
    c. 9,330
    d. 10,330

6. 4766 + 234 =
    a. 5,000
    b. 4,000
    c. 4,422
    d. 4,522

Subtraction:

7. 38
    - 17
    a. 45
    b. 55
    c. 11
    d. 21

8. 914
    - 381
    a. 633
    b. 1,295
    c. 533
    d. 523

9. 1234
    - 145
    a. 1,189
    b. 1,379
    c. 1,111
    d. 1,089

10. 321
    - 94
    a. 225
    b. 227
    c. 327
    d. 317

Carney Educational Services How to Prepare for the CAT/6

11. 119 - 107 =

   a. 22
   b. 12
   c. 16
   d. 226

12. 6257 - 5603 =

   a. 654
   b. 1,654
   c. 854
   d. 860

Multiplication:

13. 81
     x 7

   a. 567
   b. 568
   c. 637
   d. 487

14. 53
     x 5

   a. 215
   b. 265
   c. 268
   d. 315

15. 24
     x 60

   a. 1,224
   b. 1,340
   c. 1,540
   d. 1,440

16. 61
     x 49

   a. 2,899
   b. 2,424
   c. 2,989
   d. 2,900

17. 405 x 7 =

   a. 2,135
   b. 2,840
   c. 2,835
   d. 2,140

18. 458 x 86 =

   a. 40,456
   b. 40,388
   c. 39,488
   d. 39,388

Division:

Parent Tip: Make up some division problems that don't come out evenly. Make sure your student can express the answer with **a remainder** OR with **a fraction** OR as **a decimal**.

$$\begin{array}{r} 5\ R\ 3 \\ 4\overline{)23} \\ \underline{-20} \\ 3 \end{array} \qquad \begin{array}{r} 5\frac{3}{4} \\ 4\overline{)23} \\ \underline{-20} \\ 3 \end{array} \qquad \begin{array}{r} 5.75 \\ 4\overline{)23.00} \\ \underline{-20} \\ 30 \\ \underline{-28} \\ 20 \end{array}$$

19. $4\overline{)93}$

   a. 23.1
   b. 23.25
   c. 22.25
   d. 22.1

20. $7\overline{)414}$

   a. 59 R 1
   b. 59 R 7
   c. 60 R 1
   d. 60 R 7

21. $5\overline{)538}$

   a. 107.6
   b. 170.6
   c. 107.5
   d. 107.25

22. $6\overline{)260}$

   a. 42 R 6
   b. 43 R 6
   c. 43 R 2
   d. 43 R 4

6th Grade Edition

23. $416 \div 12 =$

a. $34\frac{1}{3}$
b. $34\frac{2}{3}$
c. $34\frac{1}{6}$
d. $34\frac{1}{12}$

24. $336 \div 50 =$

a. $6\frac{18}{25}$
b. $6\frac{9}{25}$
c. $6\frac{3}{4}$
d. $7\frac{18}{25}$

Decimals -

Parent Tip: When working with **adding** or **subtracting** decimals, you must make sure that the decimals are lined up and add zeros when necessary.

$34.04 + 5.2 + 12.901$

$34.04\underline{0}$ ← add a zero
$5.2\underline{00}$ ← add 2 zeros
$+12.901$

$154.3 - 63.067$

$154.3\underline{00}$ ← add 2 zeros
$\underline{-63.067}$

Addition and Subtraction:

25. $8.618 + 5.31 =$
a. 8.607
b. 8.328
c. 13.928
d. 13.649

26. $15.8 + 14.237 =$
a. 30.837
b. 30.037
c. 29.037
d. 29.837

27. $6.1 + 1.04 + 3.213 =$
a. 10.533
b. 9.353
c. 10.353
d. 9.533

28. $55.4 - 24.3 =$
a. 79.1
b. 79.7
c. 31.1
d. 30.1

29. $32.8 - 5.03 =$
a. 27.77
b. 27.11
c. 37.77
d. 37.11

30. $6.02 - 5.101 =$
a. 1.919
b. 1.909
c. 0.909
d. 0.919

Parent Tip: When working with **multiplying** decimals, there must be the same amount of digits after the decimal point in the answer as there are digits after the decimal points in the two numbers being multiplied.

$12.\underline{1}$ ← **one** digit after the decimal point
$\underline{\times\ 1.02}$ ← **two** digits after the decimal point
12.342 ← **three** digits after the decimal point

Multiplication:

31. $0.5 \times 0.3 =$
a. 1.5
b. 0.8
c. 0.08
d. 0.15

32. $1.02 \times 0.1 =$
a. 0.121
b. 0.102
c. 0.112
d. 1.12

33. $0.3 \times 0.15 =$
a. 4.5
b. 0.45
c. 0.045
d. 0.0045

34. 42.8 x 12 =

   a. 513.6
   b. 512.6
   c. 413.6
   d. 412.6

35. 9.3 x 0.7 =

   a. 6.51
   b. 6.31
   c. 5.81
   d. 5.61

36. 21.7 x 5.4 =

   a. 10.718
   b. 11.718
   c. 107.18
   d. 117.18

Parent Tip: When dividing with decimals, you must clear the decimal point in the divisor (the number dividing the other number). To do this, move the decimal point to the right until it is at the end of the number. Once you have done that, count the number of places you moved it and move the decimal in the dividend (the number being divided) the same amount of times. Now divide moving the decimal point straight up into the quotient (answer).

0.7)2.87 → the divisor, 0.7, has a decimal point and must be moved over to the right once.

↓

7)28.7 → since 0.7 became 7, 2.87 becomes 28.7 by moving the decimal point also.

The quotient (answer):   4.1
                       7)28.7

Division:

37. 1.68 ÷ 4 =

   a. 0.32
   b. 0.032
   c. 0.42
   d. 4.2

38. 7.42 ÷ 7 =

   a. 1.6
   b. 0.16
   c. 0.106
   d. 1.06

39. 39.1 ÷ 0.9 =

   a. 43.44
   b. 4.344
   c. 434.4
   d. 0.4344

40. 2.1 ÷ 0.24 =

   a. 8.75
   b. 87.5
   c. 875
   d. 8750

41. 0.36 ÷ 0.05 =

   a. 0.72
   b. 7.2
   c. 72
   d. 720

42. 48 ÷ 0.32 =

   a. 0.150
   b. 1.5
   c. 15
   d. 150

Fractions –

Parent Tip: Remember when adding or subtracting fractions, the denominators **MUST** be the same. Once you find the common denominator and change the fractions, **only add or subtract the numerators**, leaving the denominator the same. **Note:** Always Reduce Your Answer!

Addition and Subtraction:

43. $\frac{7}{5} + \frac{9}{5} =$

    a. $1\frac{2}{5}$
    b. $3\frac{1}{5}$
    c. $3\frac{1}{10}$
    d. $2\frac{1}{5}$

44. $\frac{43}{37} - \frac{15}{37} =$

    a. $\frac{28}{74}$
    b. $\frac{28}{37}$
    c. $1\frac{21}{37}$
    d. $\frac{29}{37}$

45. $\frac{3}{12} + \frac{6}{12} =$

    a. $\frac{3}{4}$
    b. $\frac{3}{12}$
    c. $\frac{1}{2}$
    d. $\frac{18}{24}$

46. $\frac{3}{4} - \frac{1}{5} =$

    a. $\frac{1}{10}$
    b. $\frac{1}{2}$
    c. $\frac{2}{5}$
    d. $\frac{11}{20}$

47. $\frac{5}{8} + \frac{5}{7} =$

    a. $1\frac{19}{56}$
    b. $1\frac{5}{56}$
    c. $\frac{19}{56}$
    d. $\frac{5}{56}$

48. $\frac{7}{8} - \frac{1}{10} =$

    a. $\frac{4}{9}$
    b. $\frac{39}{40}$
    c. $\frac{31}{40}$
    d. $\frac{1}{3}$

Parent Tip: When multiplying fractions, simply multiply numerators by numerators and denominators by denominators. **Note:** Always Reduce Your Answer!

Multiplication:

49. $\frac{4}{7} \times \frac{3}{5} =$

    a. $\frac{1}{12}$
    b. $\frac{7}{12}$
    c. $\frac{7}{35}$
    d. $\frac{12}{35}$

50. $\frac{1}{4} \times \frac{8}{11} =$

    a. $\frac{8}{15}$
    b. $\frac{7}{44}$
    c. $\frac{2}{11}$
    d. $\frac{3}{5}$

51. $\frac{1}{5} \times \frac{11}{13} =$

    a. $\frac{11}{18}$
    b. $\frac{11}{65}$
    c. $\frac{2}{3}$
    d. $\frac{12}{65}$

52. $\dfrac{5}{9} \times \dfrac{7}{10} =$

    a. $\dfrac{7}{18}$

    b. $\dfrac{12}{19}$

    c. $\dfrac{2}{3}$

    d. $\dfrac{2}{15}$

53. $\dfrac{8}{7} \times \dfrac{21}{2} =$

    a. $3\dfrac{2}{9}$

    b. 12

    c. $2\dfrac{1}{14}$

    d. $18\dfrac{2}{3}$

54. $\dfrac{6}{7} \times \dfrac{14}{27} =$

    a. $2\dfrac{1}{4}$

    b. $\dfrac{4}{9}$

    c. $\dfrac{12}{27}$

    d. $\dfrac{10}{17}$

Parent Tip: When dividing with fractions, multiply the dividend (the first fraction) by the reciprocal of the divisor (the second fraction). Reciprocal is when you turn the fraction upside down.

Note: Always Reduce Your Answer!

$$\dfrac{7}{8} \div \dfrac{3}{4} = \rightarrow \dfrac{7}{8} \times \dfrac{4}{3} = \dfrac{28}{24} = \dfrac{7}{6} = 1\dfrac{1}{6}$$

the reciprocal of $\dfrac{3}{4}$ is $\dfrac{4}{3}$

Division:

55. $\dfrac{3}{4} \div \dfrac{1}{3} =$

    a. $2\dfrac{1}{4}$

    b. $\dfrac{1}{4}$

    c. $1\dfrac{1}{2}$

    d. $2\dfrac{1}{2}$

56. $\dfrac{3}{8} \div \dfrac{3}{5} =$

    a. $\dfrac{6}{13}$

    b. $\dfrac{9}{40}$

    c. $\dfrac{5}{8}$

    d. $\dfrac{7}{8}$

57. $\dfrac{7}{12} \div \dfrac{5}{4} =$

    a. $\dfrac{7}{15}$

    b. $\dfrac{35}{48}$

    c. $\dfrac{3}{4}$

    d. $\dfrac{1}{4}$

58. $\dfrac{7}{10} \div \dfrac{7}{6} =$

    a. $\dfrac{49}{60}$

    b. $\dfrac{3}{5}$

    c. $\dfrac{4}{5}$

    d. $\dfrac{7}{30}$

59. $\dfrac{14}{15} \div \dfrac{7}{9} =$

    a. $1\dfrac{1}{9}$

    b. $\dfrac{7}{15}$

    c. $1\dfrac{1}{6}$

    d. $1\dfrac{1}{5}$

60. $\dfrac{9}{16} \div \dfrac{8}{3} =$

    a. $\dfrac{72}{48}$

    b. $1\dfrac{1}{2}$

    c. $\dfrac{27}{128}$

    d. $\dfrac{1}{2}$

Positive and Negative Numbers (Integers) –

Parent Tip: Adding numbers with the same signs (both + or both -), keep the sign the same and just add the numbers → $^-4 + ^-5 = ^-9$. When the signs are different, keep the sign of the larger number (without looking at the sign) and subtract the two numbers for the value → $^-15 + 8 = ^-7$. Since 15 is greater than 8, your answer is negative and is the difference between 15 and 8 which is 7.

Addition:

61. $^-3 + ^-7 =$
   a. $^-4$
   b. $^-10$
   c. 10
   d. 4

62. $^-23 + ^-8 =$
   a. $^-31$
   b. $^-15$
   c. 31
   d. 15

63. $^-20 + ^-40 =$
   a. 20
   b. 60
   c. $^-20$
   d. $^-60$

64. $^-15 + 13 =$
   a. $^-2$
   b. 2
   c. $^-28$
   d. 28

65. $^-43 + 61 =$
   a. $^-104$
   b. $^-18$
   c. 18
   d. 104

66. $33 + ^-74 =$
   a. 107
   b. $^-107$
   c. $^-41$
   d. 41

Parent Tip: The first thing to do with a subtraction problem is change it into an addition problem. Leave the minuend (the first number) alone, change the subtrahend (the second number) to its opposite and then add the two number applying the addition of integers rules.
$^-13 - ^-5 =$ → leave $^-13$ alone, change $^-5$ to 5,
now add the two numbers together → $^-13 + 5 = ^-8$

Subtraction:

67. $^-23 - 4 =$
   a. $^-27$
   b. $^-19$
   c. 19
   d. 27

68. $78 - ^-19 =$
   a. $^-97$
   b. 97
   c. 59
   d. $^-59$

69. $^-35 - ^-35 =$
   a. $^-70$
   b. 70
   c. 0
   d. 75

70. $^-43 - ^-17 =$
   a. 60
   b. $^-60$
   c. $^-26$
   d. 26

71. $75 - ^-22 =$
   a. 63
   b. $^-63$
   c. $^-97$
   d. 97

72. $^-56 - 34 =$
   a. $^-90$
   b. 90
   c. $^-22$
   d. 22

> **Parent Tip:** Multiplying and dividing integers has the same sign rules for the answers. If you multiply or divide numbers with the same sign, the answer will be positive.
>
> $$^-5 \times {}^-7 = 35 \quad \text{and} \quad {}^-56 \div {}^-14 = 4$$
>
> And if you multiply or divide numbers with different signs, the answer will be negative.
>
> $$^-12 \times 4 = {}^-48 \quad \text{and} \quad 63 \div {}^-9 = {}^-7$$

Multiplication:

73. $^-3 \times 6 =$
    a. 18
    b. $^-18$
    c. $^-24$
    d. 24

74. $14 \times {}^-3 =$
    a. $^-42$
    b. 42
    c. $^-52$
    d. 52

75. $^-20 \times {}^-15 =$
    a. $^-300$
    b. 300
    c. $^-400$
    d. 350

76. $13 \times 25 =$
    a. $^-350$
    b. 350
    c. $^-325$
    d. 325

77. $^-151 \times {}^-7 =$
    a. $^-757$
    b. 757
    c. $^-1057$
    d. 1057

78. $^-83 \times 16 =$
    a. 1228
    b. 1328
    c. $^-1328$
    d. $^-1228$

Division:

79. $^-125 \div 25 =$
    a. $^-5$
    b. 5
    c. $^-4$
    d. 4

80. $372 \div {}^-3 =$
    a. $^-114$
    b. 124
    c. $^-123$
    d. $^-124$

81. $^-693 \div {}^-21 =$
    a. $^-33$
    b. 33
    c. 30
    d. $^-30$

82. $^-84 \div 3 =$
    a. 26
    b. 28
    c. $^-28$
    d. $^-26$

83. $^-96 \div {}^-8 =$
    a. 11
    b. $^-11$
    c. $^-12$
    d. 12

84. $144 \div {}^-12 =$
    a. 13
    b. $^-13$
    c. 12
    d. $^-12$

Content Cluster: NUMBER SENSE

Objective: Students will be able to compare and order fractions, decimals and mixed numbers.

> **Parent Tip:** When comparing fractions, multiply the numerator (top number) of the first fraction with the denominator (bottom number) of the second fraction. Then, multiply the numerator of the second fraction with the denominator of the first fraction. If the first answer is larger, then the first fraction is larger and if smaller, then the first fraction is smaller.
>
> $$\frac{5}{7} \square \frac{4}{5}$$
>
> $5 \times 5 = 25$; $\frac{5}{7} \nwarrow \frac{4}{5}$
>
> $\frac{5}{7} \nearrow \frac{4}{5}$; $4 \times 7 = 28$
>
> Since 25 is less than 28, then $\frac{5}{7} < \frac{4}{5}$

Compare the following fractions:

1. $\frac{7}{8} \square \frac{9}{11}$

    a. <
    b. =
    c. >

2. $\frac{6}{7} \square \frac{12}{13}$

    a. <
    b. =
    c. >

3. $\frac{8}{9} \square \frac{2}{3}$

    a. <
    b. =
    c. >

4. $\frac{5}{15} \square \frac{1}{3}$

    a. <
    b. =
    c. >

5. $\frac{13}{14} \square \frac{4}{5}$

    a. <
    b. =
    c. >

6. $\frac{1}{3} \square \frac{1}{2}$

    a. <
    b. =
    c. >

Parent Tip: When comparing decimals, make sure you have the same amount of places after the decimal point in each number. Then you can compare the numbers much easier.

Example: 0.06 ☐ 0.056
0.0<u>60</u>   0.0<u>56</u>
Since 60 is greater than 56, then 0.06 > 0.056

Compare the following decimals:

7. 0.4 ☐ 0.35
   a. <
   b. =
   c. >

8. 0.07 ☐ 0.6
   a. <
   b. =
   c. >

9. 0.81 ☐ 0.810
   a. <
   b. =
   c. >

10. 0.34 ☐ 0.304
    a. <
    b. =
    c. >

11. 1.02 ☐ 1.2
    a. <
    b. =
    c. >

12. 3.15 ☐ 3.150
    a. <
    b. =
    c. >

Parent Tip: Change the mixed numbers into improper fractions and then compare as fractions.

$$2\frac{1}{2} \square 2\frac{1}{5}$$

$$\frac{5}{2} \square \frac{11}{5}$$

Note: To change a mixed number into an improper fraction, multiply the whole number by the denominator and add the numerator:

Example - $2\frac{1}{2}$; (2 × 2) + 1 = 5 becoming the improper fraction $\frac{5}{2}$

then cross multiply; 25 > 22; since 25 is greater than 22, then $2\frac{1}{2} > 2\frac{1}{5}$

Compare the following mixed numbers:

13. $1\frac{1}{4}$ ☐ $1\frac{1}{2}$
    a. <
    b. =
    c. >

14. $4\frac{1}{5}$ ☐ $4\frac{2}{10}$
    a. <
    b. =
    c. >

15. $3\frac{3}{7}$ ☐ $3\frac{1}{2}$
    a. <
    b. =
    c. >

16. $5\frac{3}{4}$ ☐ $5\frac{3}{5}$
    a. <
    b. =
    c. >

Parent Tip: When putting fractions in order, find a common denominator, change all the fractions to the same common denominator, then put in order by the value of the numerators. With decimals, line up the decimals, add zeros where needed, then put in order by the new number values.

Example: $\frac{1}{2}, \frac{3}{4}, \frac{3}{8}$; the common denominator is 8

$\frac{4}{8}, \frac{6}{8}, \frac{3}{8}$

Put in order from least to greatest: $\frac{3}{8}, \frac{1}{2}, \frac{3}{4}$

Example: 0.04, 0.4, 0.044

0.04<u>0</u> - add one zero
0.4<u>00</u> - add two zeros
0.044

Put in order from least to greatest: 0.040, 0.044, 0.400

Put in order from least to greatest:

17. 0.107, 0.79, 0.45

   a. 0.107, 0.79, 0.45
   b. 0.79, 0.107, 0.45
   c. 0.107, 0.45, 0.79
   d. 0.79, 0.45, 0.107

18. 0.1, 0.01, 0.11

   a. 0.01, 0.1, 0.11
   b. 0.11, 0.1, 0.01
   c. 0.01, 0.11, 0.1
   d. 0.1, 0.11, 0.01

19. $\frac{1}{2}, \frac{1}{4}, \frac{1}{3}$

   a. $\frac{1}{2}, \frac{1}{3}, \frac{1}{4}$
   b. $\frac{1}{4}, \frac{1}{2}, \frac{1}{3}$
   c. $\frac{1}{3}, \frac{1}{4}, \frac{1}{2}$
   d. $\frac{1}{4}, \frac{1}{3}, \frac{1}{2}$

Put in order from greatest to least:

20. 1.001, 1.01, 1.002

   a. 1.01, 1.001, 1.002
   b. 1.002, 1.01, 1.001
   c. 1.01, 1.002, 1.001
   d. 1.001, 1.002, 1.01

21. 0.0303, 0.3, 0.033

   a. 0.0303, 0.3, 0.033
   b. 0.033, 0.0303, 0.3
   c. 0.0303, 0.033, 0.3
   d. 0.3, 0.033, 0.0303

22. $\frac{7}{8}, \frac{2}{3}, \frac{4}{5}$

   a. $\frac{7}{8}, \frac{2}{3}, \frac{4}{5}$
   b. $\frac{2}{3}, \frac{4}{5}, \frac{7}{8}$
   c. $\frac{4}{5}, \frac{7}{8}, \frac{2}{3}$
   d. $\frac{7}{8}, \frac{4}{5}, \frac{2}{3}$

Parent Tip: Make sure the student knows in which order is wanted: Do they want **Least** to **Greatest**? or Do they want **Greatest** to **Least**?

Content Cluster: NUMBER SENSE

Objective: Students will solve problems involving fractions, ratios, proportions and percentages.

> **Parent Tip:** When working with any type of word problem, make sure you know what the question is asking and once you get your answer, re-read the question and make sure your answer **fits the question!**

Fraction Problems:

1. John worked out at the gym for $3\frac{3}{4}$ hours. Jamal worked out for $4\frac{1}{2}$ hours. How much longer did Jamal work out than John?

    a. $\frac{1}{2}$ hour
    b. $\frac{2}{3}$ hour
    c. $\frac{3}{4}$ hour
    d. $\frac{1}{6}$ hour

2. Judy, Jose and Barbara all worked at the same book store. Judy worked for $2\frac{1}{2}$ hours, Jose worked for $2\frac{2}{3}$ hours and Barbara worked for $2\frac{5}{6}$ hours on Saturday. What was the total amount of hours they worked Saturday?

    a. $5\frac{5}{6}$ hours
    b. 6 hours
    c. $7\frac{11}{12}$ hours
    d. 8 hours

3. One meter of steel wire costs $8\frac{1}{4}$ cents. How much would it cost for 12 meters of steel wire?

    a. 84 cents
    b. 96 cents
    c. 90 cents
    d. 99 cents

4. Lim practices her trumpet $1\frac{1}{2}$ hours per day. After how many days has she spent 24 hours practicing?

    a. 24 days
    b. 16 days
    c. 14 days
    d. 30 days

Carney Educational Services   How to Prepare for the CAT/6

5. In Ms Johnson's 6th grade class, $\frac{1}{3}$ of the students are in the band club, $\frac{1}{6}$ are in the jump rope club and $\frac{1}{5}$ are in the chess club. How many of the 30 students in class are **not** in one of those clubs?

    a. 21 students   c. 27 students
    b. 9 students   d. 16 students

6. One pound of peanuts costs 96 cents. How much would it cost for $\frac{5}{8}$ pound of peanuts?

    a. 50 cents   c. 60 cents
    b. 65 cents   d. 75 cents

> **Parent Tip:** a ratio compares one quantity with another and can be expressed as a **fraction**, using a **division sign** or a **colon** (ratio sign).
>
> Example: $\frac{3}{5}$ → $3 \div 5$ → 3:5 <u>all three</u> represent the same ratio.

<u>Write as a ratio:</u>

7. There are 14 boys and 12 girls in the Music Club. What is the ratio of boys to girls?

    a. 14 ÷ 12   c. 14 ÷ 26
    b. 12 ÷ 14   d. 12 ÷ 26

8. There are 15 dogs and 20 cats in the Pet Store. What is the ratio of cats to dogs?

    a. 20:35   c. 20:15
    b. 15:35   d. 15:20

9. Strawberries are selling at a rate of 98 cents for 2 boxes. What is the ratio of the cost of 6 boxes of strawberries?

    a. 6 boxes / $5.88   c. $2.94 / 6 boxes
    b. $5.88 / 6 boxes   d. 6 boxes / $2.94

6th Grade Edition

10. Oranges cost $1.25 per dozen. What is the ratio of the cost of 2 dozen oranges?

    a. $2.50 / 2 dozen   c. $3.75 / 2 dozen

    b. 2 dozen / $2.50   d. 2 dozen / $3.75

Parent Tip: A proportion is a statement two equal ratios: $\dfrac{7}{8} = \dfrac{12}{16}$

When solving a proportion, you cross product (making an equation) and then you solve for the unknown.

Example: $\dfrac{n}{4} = \dfrac{12}{16} \rightarrow \dfrac{n}{4} \times \dfrac{12}{16} \rightarrow 16n = 48 \rightarrow \dfrac{16n}{16} = \dfrac{48}{16} \rightarrow n = 3$

                                                                                             (equation)

Solve the proportions:

11. $\dfrac{n}{8} = \dfrac{9}{24}$

    a. 72
    b. 3
    c. 24
    d. 5

12. $\dfrac{12}{3} = \dfrac{x}{12}$

    a. 48
    b. 144
    c. 36
    d. 4

13. $\dfrac{8}{5} = \dfrac{24}{y}$

    a. 3
    b. 40
    c. 15
    d. 120

14. $\dfrac{2}{p} = \dfrac{18}{27}$

    a. 36
    b. 9
    c. 3
    d. 54

15. $\dfrac{d}{5} = \dfrac{3}{4}$

    a. 2
    b. 2.5
    c. 4
    d. 3.75

16. $\dfrac{5}{6} = \dfrac{3}{c}$

    a. 3.6
    b. 4
    c. 4.5
    d. 5

> **Parent Tip:** Any time you are working with a percent word problem, you can set it up as a proportion problem:
>
> $$\frac{\%}{100} = \frac{\text{"is"}}{\text{"of"}}$$
>
> In the proportion → % = the percent number
> 100 = will always be there, **leave it alone**
> "is" = the number **before** the word "is" goes there
> "of" = the number **after** the "of" goes there
>
> **Note:** one of the three (%,is,of) will be missing, put an **n** in that place)
>
> Example: 25 is **what percent** of 50. → $\frac{n}{100} = \frac{25}{50}$ → 50n = 2500 → n = **50%**
>
> Notice that the %→n, the "is"→25, the "of"→50 and the 100 stayed the same. The answer fits the question.

Find the percent or number:

17. What is 12% of 50?
    a. 12
    b. 6
    c. 25
    d. 3

18. 30 is what percent of 50?
    a. 25%
    b. 30%
    c. 60%
    d. 50%

19. 10 is 20% of what number?
    a. 10
    b. 20
    c. 30
    d. 50

20. 48 is what percent of 80?
    a. 40%
    b. 50%
    c. 60%
    d. 80%

21. 24 is 40% of what number?
    a. 6
    b. 40
    c. 48
    d. 60

22. What is 80% of 80?
    a. 48
    b. 64
    c. 72
    d. 76

Carney Educational Services How to Prepare for the CAT/6

Content Cluster: NUMBER SENSE

Objective: Students will calculate and solve problems involving addition, subtraction, multiplication and division of rational numbers.

> **Parent Tip:** The definition of a rational number is any number that can be represented in the $\frac{a}{b}$ form of two integers a and b, b can **not** be zero.

Addition and Subtraction:

> **Parent Tip:** Remember when **adding** or **subtracting** rational numbers, the denominators must be the same and the rules for adding (subtracting) integers also apply.
> $$\frac{^-2}{5} + \frac{3}{4} \rightarrow \frac{^-8}{20} + \frac{15}{20} = \frac{7}{20}$$

1. $\dfrac{7}{5} + \dfrac{^-3}{5} =$

    a. $\dfrac{4}{10}$
    b. $\dfrac{4}{5}$
    c. $\dfrac{^-4}{5}$
    d. $\dfrac{^-4}{10}$

2. $\dfrac{^-5}{37} - \dfrac{15}{37} =$

    a. $\dfrac{10}{37}$
    b. $\dfrac{20}{37}$
    c. $\dfrac{^-10}{37}$
    d. $\dfrac{^-20}{37}$

3. $\dfrac{^-3}{12} + \dfrac{^-4}{12} =$

    a. $\dfrac{7}{12}$
    b. $\dfrac{1}{12}$
    c. $\dfrac{^-7}{12}$
    d. $\dfrac{^-1}{12}$

4. $\dfrac{7}{15} - \dfrac{^-2}{15} =$

    a. $\dfrac{^-2}{3}$
    b. $\dfrac{2}{3}$
    c. $\dfrac{3}{5}$
    d. $\dfrac{^-3}{5}$

5. $\dfrac{^-1}{2} + \dfrac{1}{3} =$

    a. $\dfrac{1}{6}$
    b. $\dfrac{^-1}{6}$
    c. $\dfrac{1}{5}$
    d. $\dfrac{^-1}{5}$

6. $\dfrac{^-3}{4} - \dfrac{^-1}{2} =$

    a. $^-1\dfrac{1}{4}$
    b. $\dfrac{^-2}{3}$
    c. $\dfrac{1}{4}$
    d. $\dfrac{^-1}{4}$

6th Grade Edition

7. $\dfrac{-3}{8} + \dfrac{-1}{5} =$

    a. $\dfrac{23}{40}$

    b. $\dfrac{-4}{13}$

    c. $\dfrac{-23}{40}$

    d. $\dfrac{-2}{13}$

8. $\dfrac{3}{8} - \dfrac{1}{3} =$

    a. $\dfrac{2}{5}$

    b. $\dfrac{-2}{5}$

    c. $\dfrac{17}{24}$

    d. $\dfrac{-17}{24}$

9. $\dfrac{-7}{8} - \dfrac{-1}{4} =$

    a. $\dfrac{-5}{8}$

    b. $\dfrac{5}{8}$

    c. $\dfrac{-2}{3}$

    d. $\dfrac{2}{3}$

Multiplication:

> **Parent Tip:** When **multiplying** rational numbers, multiply numerator by numerator and denominator by denominator.
> **Remember:**   Positive x Positive = Positive
>   Negative x Negative = Positive
>   Positive x Negative = Negative
>   Negative x Positive = Negative
>
> $$\dfrac{-1}{5} \times \dfrac{2}{3} = \dfrac{-1 \times 2}{5 \times 3} = \dfrac{-2}{15}$$

10. $\dfrac{3}{7} \times \dfrac{-3}{4} =$

    a. $\dfrac{6}{11}$

    b. $\dfrac{-6}{11}$

    c. $\dfrac{-9}{28}$

    d. $\dfrac{9}{28}$

11. $\dfrac{-1}{4} \times \dfrac{-3}{11} =$

    a. $\dfrac{1}{11}$

    b. $\dfrac{3}{44}$

    c. $\dfrac{-3}{44}$

    d. $\dfrac{-4}{15}$

12. $\dfrac{-1}{5} \times \dfrac{3}{7} =$

    a. $\dfrac{-3}{35}$

    b. $\dfrac{3}{35}$

    c. $\dfrac{2}{35}$

    d. $\dfrac{-1}{3}$

13. $\dfrac{-4}{9} \times \dfrac{-1}{5} =$

   a. $\dfrac{-4}{45}$

   b. $\dfrac{4}{45}$

   c. $\dfrac{-5}{14}$

   d. $\dfrac{3}{4}$

14. $\dfrac{-8}{7} \times \dfrac{5}{3} =$

   a. $-1\dfrac{19}{21}$

   b. $1\dfrac{19}{21}$

   c. $-1\dfrac{3}{10}$

   d. $\dfrac{-3}{4}$

15. $\dfrac{6}{7} \times \dfrac{-2}{3} =$

   a. $\dfrac{4}{7}$

   b. $\dfrac{-4}{7}$

   c. $\dfrac{4}{5}$

   d. $\dfrac{-4}{5}$

Division:

Parent Tip: When **dividing** rational numbers, multiply the first fraction by the reciprocal (turn the fraction upside down) of the second fraction.

$\dfrac{2}{5} \div \dfrac{-3}{4}$, since $\dfrac{-4}{3}$ is the reciprocal of $\dfrac{-3}{4}$ then; $\dfrac{2}{5} \times \dfrac{-4}{3} = \dfrac{-8}{15}$

16. $\dfrac{-3}{2} \div \dfrac{1}{4} =$

   a. -6

   b. 6

   c. $\dfrac{-3}{8}$

   d. $\dfrac{3}{8}$

17. $\dfrac{-3}{8} \div \dfrac{-6}{5} =$

   a. $\dfrac{-9}{13}$

   b. $\dfrac{-5}{16}$

   c. $\dfrac{5}{16}$

   d. $\dfrac{9}{13}$

18. $\dfrac{7}{12} \div \dfrac{-5}{4} =$

   a. $\dfrac{-7}{15}$

   b. $\dfrac{7}{15}$

   c. $\dfrac{-3}{4}$

   d. $\dfrac{3}{8}$

19. $\dfrac{-7}{10} \div \dfrac{-7}{6} =$

   a. $\dfrac{3}{5}$ c. $\dfrac{-7}{8}$

   b. $\dfrac{-3}{5}$ d. $\dfrac{7}{8}$

20. $\dfrac{-14}{15} \div \dfrac{7}{9} =$

   a. $-1\dfrac{1}{6}$ c. $1\dfrac{1}{5}$

   b. $1\dfrac{1}{6}$ d. $-1\dfrac{1}{5}$

Parent Tip: Remember, always **reduce** the answers to the lowest term!

Content Cluster: ALGEBRA AND FUNCTIONS

Objective: Students will write verbal expressions and sentences as algebraic expressions and sentences.

> Parent Tip: Know what each word is as a symbol, i.e. "is → =", "the sum → +", "the product → x", etc

Word to symbol list:

Addition (+)	Subtraction (−)	Multiplication (x)	Division (÷)
the <u>sum</u> of	the <u>difference</u> of (when)	the <u>product</u> of (when)	the <u>quotient</u> of (when)
the <u>total</u> of	<u>less</u> than	<u>times</u>	<u>divided</u> by
<u>added</u> to	<u>smaller</u> than	<u>multiplied</u> by	
<u>increased</u> by	<u>subtracted</u> from		
<u>greater</u> than	<u>decreased</u> by		
<u>larger</u> than			

Write as algebraic expressions:

> **Parent Tip:** Algebraic expressions **do not** have a mathematical verb, that is one of the symbols =, <, or >

1. The product of seven and n
    a. 7 + n
    b. n - 7
    c. 7n
    d. 7 ÷ n

2. Eleven larger than x
    a. x + 11
    b. 11 - x
    c. 11x
    d. 11 ÷ x

3. The quotient when b is divided by five
    a. b + 5
    b. b - 5
    c. 5b
    d. b ÷ 5

4. Twelve less than w
    a. w + 12
    b. w - 12
    c. 12w
    d. 12 ÷ w

5. The sum of six and g
    a. 6 + g
    b. 6 - g
    c. 6g
    d. 6 ÷ g

6. t increased by ten
    a. t + 10
    b. t - 10
    c. 10t
    d. t ÷ 10

7. Nine times a
    a. 9 + a
    b. 9 - a
    c. 9a
    d. 9 ÷ a

8. Twenty-five divided by d
    a. 25 + d
    b. 25 - d
    c. 25d
    d. 25 ÷ d

9. Total of three and p
    a. 3 + p
    b. 3 - p
    c. 3p
    d. 3 ÷ p

Write as algebraic sentences:

> **Parent Tip:** Algebraic sentences **must have** a mathematical verb, that is one of the symbols =, <, or >

10. Three greater than y is fifteen.

    a. $y + 3 = 15$
    b. $y - 3 = 15$
    c. $3y = 15$
    d. $y \div 3 = 15$

11. Two less than m is eleven.

    a. $m + 2 = 11$
    b. $m - 2 = 11$
    c. $2m = 11$
    d. $m \div 2 = 11$

12. The difference between h and five is thirty.

    a. $h + 5 = 30$
    b. $h - 5 = 30$
    c. $5h = 30$
    d. $h \div 5 = 30$

13. The total of k and forty is sixty.

    a. $k + 40 = 60$
    b. $k - 40 = 60$
    c. $40k = 60$
    d. $k \div 40 = 60$

14. The product of two and x is sixteen.

    a. $x + 2 = 16$
    b. $x - 2 = 16$
    c. $2x = 16$
    d. $x \div 2 = 16$

15. The quotient when eighteen is divided by g is six.

    a. $18 + g = 6$
    b. $18 - g = 6$
    c. $18g = 6$
    d. $18 \div g = 6$

16. The sum of t and twenty is thirty-four.

    a. $t + 20 = 34$
    b. $t - 20 = 34$
    c. $20t = 34$
    d. $20 \div t = 34$

17. Fifteen decreased by n is seven.

    a. $15 + n = 7$
    b. $15 - n = 7$
    c. $15n = 7$
    d. $15 \div n = 7$

18. Seventy-five times y is one hundred fifty.

    a. $75 + y = 150$
    b. $75 - y = 150$
    c. $75y = 150$
    d. $y \div 75 = 150$

Content Cluster: ALGEBRA AND FUNCTIONS

Objective: Students will evaluate algebraic expressions.

> **Parent Tip:** When evaluating, replace <u>all</u> variables with their numerical value then do all the operations you can following the order of operations.
> **Note:** Two or more letters next to each other **or** a number and letters next to each other **means to multiply the values.** If a = 2 and b = 3 then 4ab = 4 x 2 x 3 = 24

For problems 1-6, evaluate each expression when x = 3 and y = 5

1. xy
   a. 53
   b. 15
   c. 25
   d. 35

2. y + x
   a. 8
   b. 15
   c. 2
   d. 7

3. 2x − y
   a. 8
   b. 15
   c. 1
   d. 7

4. 2y − x
   a. 13
   b. 22
   c. 7
   d. 1

5. 3x + 1 + y
   a. 15
   b. 39
   c. 14
   d. 11

6. xy − 5
   a. 13
   b. 20
   c. 48
   d. 10

For problems 7-12, evaluate each expression when a = 2, b = 7 and c = 6.

7. 3ab + 6
   a. 36
   b. 18
   c. 333
   d. 48

8. 5ab
   a. 527
   b. 70
   c. 14
   d. 45

9. $\dfrac{c}{a} + b$
   a. 10
   b. 19
   c. 44
   d. 4

10. $\dfrac{2b}{a}$
    a. 13
    b. 6
    c. 7
    d. 11

11. $\dfrac{3c}{a} - b$
    a. 2
    b. 11
    c. 3
    d. 16

12. 2a + 3b + 4c
    a. 43
    b. 49
    c. 105
    d. 24

Content Cluster: ALGEBRA AND FUNCTIONS

Objective: Students will solve simple linear equations.

Addition and subtraction equations, solve for the variable:

Parent Tip: Steps to solve addition and subtraction equations:

A. $n + 2 = 4$
    $n + 2 - 2 = 4 - 2$ → subtract 2 from both sides
    $n + 0 = 2$
    $n = 2$

B. $n - 2 = 4$
    $n + 2 + 2 = 4 + 2$ → add 2 to both sides
    $n + 0 = 6$
    $n = 6$

---

1. $a + 3 = 11$
   a. 10
   b. 9
   c. 8
   d. 14

2. $b - 10 = 1$
   a. 8
   b. 11
   c. 9
   d. 7

3. $c + 2 = 6$
   a. 2
   b. 4
   c. 8
   d. 10

4. $d - 14 = 3$
   a. 17
   b. 16
   c. 11
   d. 10

5. $18 + h = 37$
   a. 9
   b. 55
   c. 18
   d. 19

6. $m - 46 = 58$
   a. 11
   b. 12
   c. 104
   d. 102

7. $39.2 + n = 56.3$
   a. 95.5
   b. 85.5
   c. 27.1
   d. 17.1

8. $p - 3.33 = 6.67$
   a. 3.34
   b. 9
   c. 10
   d. 11

9. $q + 84.32 = 100$
   a. 15.68
   b. 26.78
   c. 184.32
   d. 174.32

Multiplication equations, solve for the variable:

> **Parent Tips:** Steps to solve multiplication equations:
> $$2n = 4$$
> $$\frac{2n}{2} = \frac{4}{2} \rightarrow \text{divide both sides by 2}$$
> $$n = 2$$

10. $5a = 35$
    a. 175
    b. 7
    c. 5
    d. 140

11. $12b = 144$
    a. 24
    b. 11
    c. 12
    d. 1444

12. $28c = 7$
    a. 4
    b. $\frac{1}{4}$
    c. $\frac{1}{2}$
    d. 2

13. $10.4d = 5.2$
    a. 2.5
    b. 0.5
    c. 0.25
    d. 5

14. $1.4f = 7$
    a. 4
    b. 5.6
    c. 0.5
    d. 5

15. $3.2g = 320$
    a. 100
    b. 10
    c. 0.1
    d. 0.01

16. $46h = 2$
    a. $\frac{1}{23}$
    b. 276
    c. 40
    d. 1

17. $23k = 1$
    a. 1
    b. 23
    c. $\frac{1}{23}$
    d. 22

18. $52m = 52$
    a. 0
    b. $\frac{1}{23}$
    c. 1
    d. $\frac{1}{20}$

Division equations, solve for the variable:

> **Parent Tips:** Steps to solve division equations:
>
> $$\frac{n}{2} = 4$$
>
> $(2)\frac{n}{2} = 4(2)$ → multiply both sides by 2
>
> $n = 8$

19. $\frac{a}{5} = 6$

   a. 30
   b. 35
   c. 4
   d. 3

20. $\frac{b}{6} = 24$

   a. 12
   b. 4
   c. 144
   d. 168

21. $\frac{c}{15} = 15$

   a. 15
   b. 125
   c. 225
   d. 1

22. $\frac{n}{0.4} = 8$

   a. 0.32
   b. 3.2
   c. 32
   d. 320

23. $\frac{p}{0.12} = 4.1$

   a. 4.92
   b. 0.492
   c. 4.92
   d. 492

24. $\frac{q}{1.25} = 0.04$

   a. 50
   b. 5
   c. 0.5
   d. 0.05

25. $\frac{r}{2} = 0.4$

   a. 0.8
   b. 0.2
   c. 2
   d. 8

26. $\frac{s}{3} = 0.06$

   a. 0.2
   b. 0.02
   c. 0.12
   d. 0.18

27. $\frac{t}{4} = 0.04$

   a. 0.3
   b. 0.12
   c. 0.16
   d. 0.01

Content Cluster: ALGEBRA AND FUNCTIONS

Objective: Students will analyze and use tables, graphs and rules to solve problems involving rates and proportions.

One Day sales of the Down Home Market (in dollars)

Use the graph above to answer questions 1 – 4:

1. What were the sales in meat for the day?

   a. $500
   b. $700
   c. $800
   d. $400

2. What were the total sales of all departments?

   a. $1600
   b. $1900
   c. $2000
   d. $2400

3. What percent of the total sales were dairy?

   a. 60%
   b. $66.\overline{6}$%
   c. $33.\overline{3}$%
   d. $16.\overline{6}$%

4. What percent of the total sales were product and grocery?

   a. 50%
   b. 60%
   c. 70%
   d. 80%

Use the information below to answer questions 5 – 7:

At the Express Airport Parking lot, the rate for parking is $3.00 for the first hour and $2.00 for each additional hour or any part of an hour. The maximum cost for one day (24 hrs) is $20.00.

5. How much would it cost to park for 6 hrs?

   a. $12.00
   b. $13.00
   c. $15.00
   d. $18.00

6. How much would it cost to park of 3 ½ hrs?

   a. $6.00
   b. $8.00
   c. $9.00
   d. $10.00

7. How much would it cost to park for 24 hrs?

   a. $15.00
   b. $20.00
   c. $40.00
   d. $49.00

Population Growth of Elm City

Year	1900	1910	1920	1930	1940	1950	1960	1970	1980	1990
Population	3,000	4,500	5,000	6,000	7,500	8,500	12,000	15,000	17,000	20,000

Use the chart above to answer questions 8 – 11:

8. Between which ten-year period did Elm City grow the most?

    a. 1910 – 1920
    b. 1930 – 1940
    c. 1950 – 1960
    d. 1970 – 1980

9. Between which ten-year period did Elm City grow the least?

    a. 1910 – 1920
    b. 1930 – 1940
    c. 1950 – 1960
    d. 1970 – 1980

10. What was the percent of increase in the population from 1900 – 1930 in Elm City?

    a. 60%
    b. 80%
    c. 100%
    d. 120%

11. Which 2 ten-year periods had the same growth rate in Elm City?

    a. 1900-1910 and 1920-1930
    b. 1900-1910 and 1930-1940
    c. 1920-1930 and 1950-1960
    d. 1940-1950 and 1980-1990

Content Cluster: ALGEBRA AND FUNCTIONS

Objective: Students will investigate geometric patterns and describe them algebraically.

> **Parent Tip:** When working with geometric patterns, look at the number of objects in the figure and try to relate that number to the position of the figure. This way you can let the algebraic formula relate to the figure location.
>
> Example:
>
> Figure 1   Figure 2   Figure 3
> (2 circles)   (4 circles)   (6 circles)
>
> Since figure 1 has 2 circles, figure 2 has 4 circles and figure 3 has 6 circles, a pattern can be established based on the figure number (position). Let **n = the figure number** and the algebraic formula would be **2n = the number of circles** in that figure so the 10th figure would have 20 circles.

Use the following figures to answer questions 1 and 2:

Figure 1   Figure 2   Figure 3   Figure 4   Figure 5

1. Which describes the geometric pattern algebraically to determine the number of squares in the figure? (n = the figure number)

   a. n + 2
   b. n^2
   c. n ÷ 2
   d. n + n

2. How many squares will there be in the 10th figure?

   a. 64
   b. 81
   c. 100
   d. 121

6th Grade Edition   91

Use the following figures to answer questions 3 and 4:

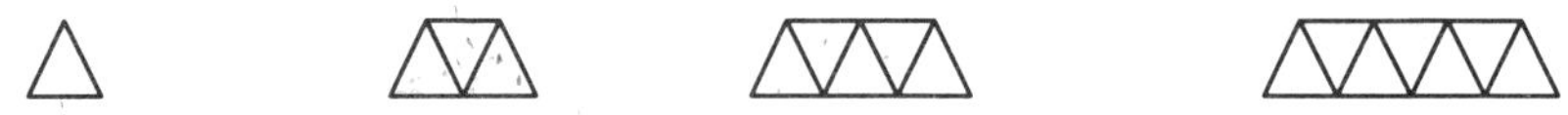

figure 1　　figure 2　　figure 3　　figure 4

3. Which describes the geometric pattern algebraically to determine the number of triangles in the figure? (n = the figure number)

    a. n + (n – 1)　　　c. n²
    b. n + n　　　　　d. n + (n + 1)

4. How many triangles will there be in the 7th figure?

    a. 15　　　c. 13
    b. 20　　　d. 12

Use the following figures to answer questions 5 and 6:

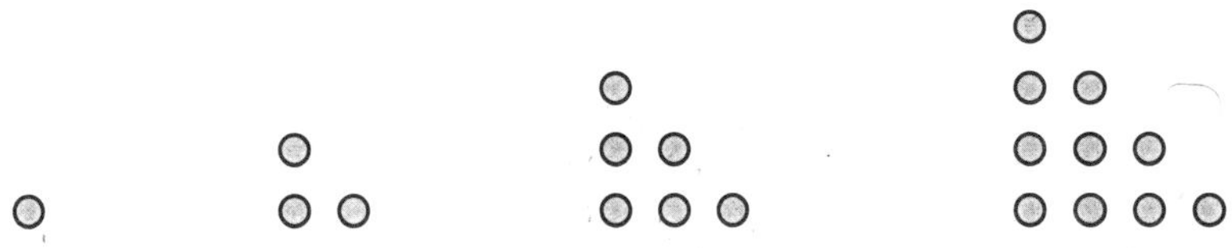

figure 1　　figure 2　　figure 3　　figure 4

5. Which describes the geometric pattern algebraically to determine the number of dots in the figure? (n = the figure number)

    a. n + (n – 1)　　　c. n² + n
    b. $\dfrac{n+n}{2}$　　　d. $\dfrac{(n)(n+1)}{2}$

6. How many triangles will there be in the 8th figure?

    a. 8　　　c. 36
    b. 15　　d. 72

Carney Educational Services How to Prepare for the CAT/6

Content Cluster: MEASUREMENT AND GEOMETRY

Objective: Students will deepen their understanding of plane and solid shapes and use this understanding to solve problems.

> **Parent Tip:** If you are working with unusual geometric shapes, break them into commonly known shapes.
>
> Example:
>
> To find the area of the figure, divide the figure into two rectangles, find their areas and add them together.

Before we start this cluster, it is important to review some of the definitions and formulas that need to be used to be successful:

Definitions:
   Perimeter of a polygon – the distance around the figure, in other words, add up all the measurements of the sides.
   Area of a polygon – the number of square units inside the polygon.

Formulas:

Area of a Triangle — $A = \dfrac{b \cdot h}{2}$ Area of a Circle — $A = \pi r^2$

Area of a Square — $A = b \cdot h$ Area of a Rectangle — $A = b \cdot h$

Area of a Rhombus — $A = b \cdot h$ Area of a Parallelogram — $A = b \cdot h$

Area of a Trapezoid — $A = \dfrac{(b_1 + b_2) h}{2}$ Circumference of a Circle — $C = \pi d$

Use the following figure to answer questions 1-2:

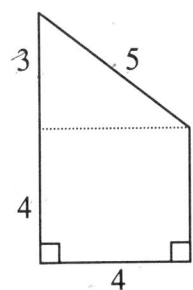

1. Find the perimeter of the figure.

   a. 13   c. 18
   b. 16   d. 20

2. Find the area of the figure.

   a. 18   c. 31
   b. 22   d. 35

6th Grade Edition

Use the following figure to answer questions 3-4:

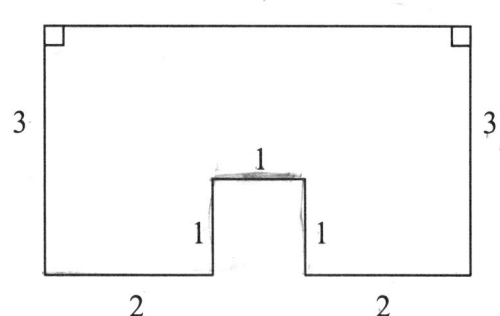

3. Find the perimeter of the figure.

   a. 13 c. 18
   b. 16 d. 20

4. Find the area of the figure.

   a. 14 c. 15
   b. 15 d. 18

Use the following figure to answer questions 5-6:

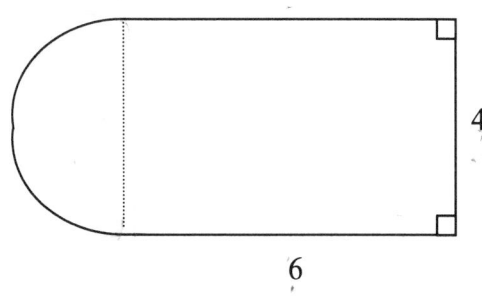

5. Find the perimeter of the figure. (use $\pi = 3.14$)

   a. 16.28 c. 28.28
   b. 22.28 d. 22.56

6. Find the area of the figure. (use $\pi = 3.14$)

   a. 22.28 c. 32.28
   b. 30.28 d. 36.28

Use the following figure to answer questions 7:

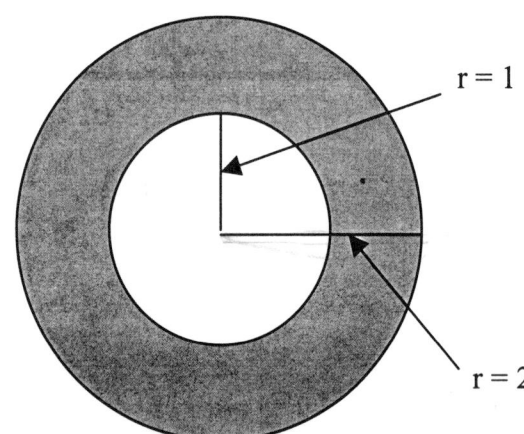

7. Find the shaded area of the circle. (use $\pi = 3.14$)

   a. 9.42   c. 15.7
   b. 12.56 d. 3.14

> **Parent Tip:** When we are working with solid shapes, they are **prisms** and **pyramids**.
>
> **Prism** – a three-dimensional figure that has two bases.
>
>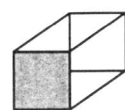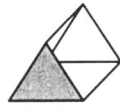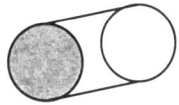
>
> **Pyramid** – a three-dimensional figure with one base.
>
>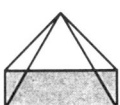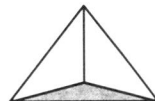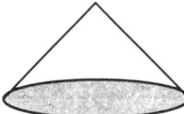

Definitions:
Base – the polygons in a prism that are the same shape opposite each other.
   Their bases name prisms and pyramids, i.e. a **triangular prism** has 2 triangle bases.
Height – the height of a prism is the distance between the 2 bases and the height of a pyramid is the distance between point and the base.
Volume – the volume of a solid figure is the number of cubic units inside.

Formulas:
Volume of a Prism – $V = Bh$ (B = the base area)

Volume of a Pyramid – $V = \frac{1}{3}Bh$ (B = the base area)

Base Area – the area of the base. Use the area formulas for polygons to get the base area.

8. Find the volume.

   a. 16
   b. 64
   c. 48
   d. 24

9. Find the volume. (use π = 3.14)

   a. 14
   b. 28
   c. 21.98
   d. 43.98

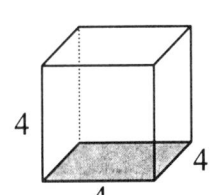

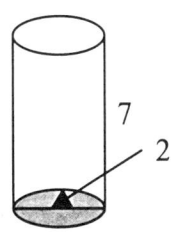

10. Find the volume.

    a. 36
    b. 48
    c. 72
    d. 78

11. Find the volume.

    a. 14
    b. 28
    c. 32
    d. 64

12. Find the volume. (use π = 3.14)

   a. 15
   b. 15.42
   c. 94.2
   d. 47.1

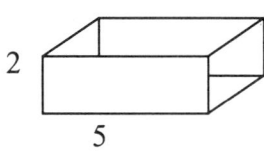

13. Find the volume. (**B** = 10)

   a. 8
   b. 12
   c. 16
   d. 20

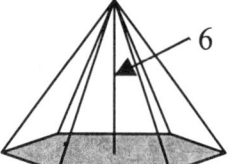

Parent Tip: When working with **surface area**, you need to find all the areas of all the faces (flat surfaces) of the prism. The area formulas are used so make sure you revisit them.

Example:

2 x (2 x 5) = 20
2 x (2 x 3) = 12
+ 2 x (3 x 5) = 30
62

There are **two** faces **2 x 5** – (front and back)

There are **two** faces **2 x 3** – (the two sides)

There are **two** faces **3 x 5** – (top and bottom)

14. Find the surface area.

   a. 60
   b. 84
   c. 96
   d. 112

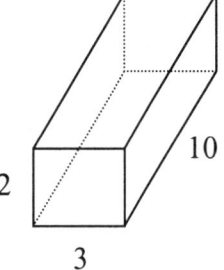

15. Find the surface area.

   a. 216
   b. 240
   c. 360
   d. 400

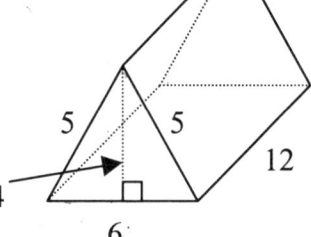

Content Cluster: MEASUREMENT AND GEOMETRY

Objective: Students will identify and describe the properties of two-dimensional figures.

Parent tip: An important element in being successful in geometry is the understanding of the definitions and putting a picture of figures in your mind. Also knowing that each figure has formulas related to it.

Definitions:

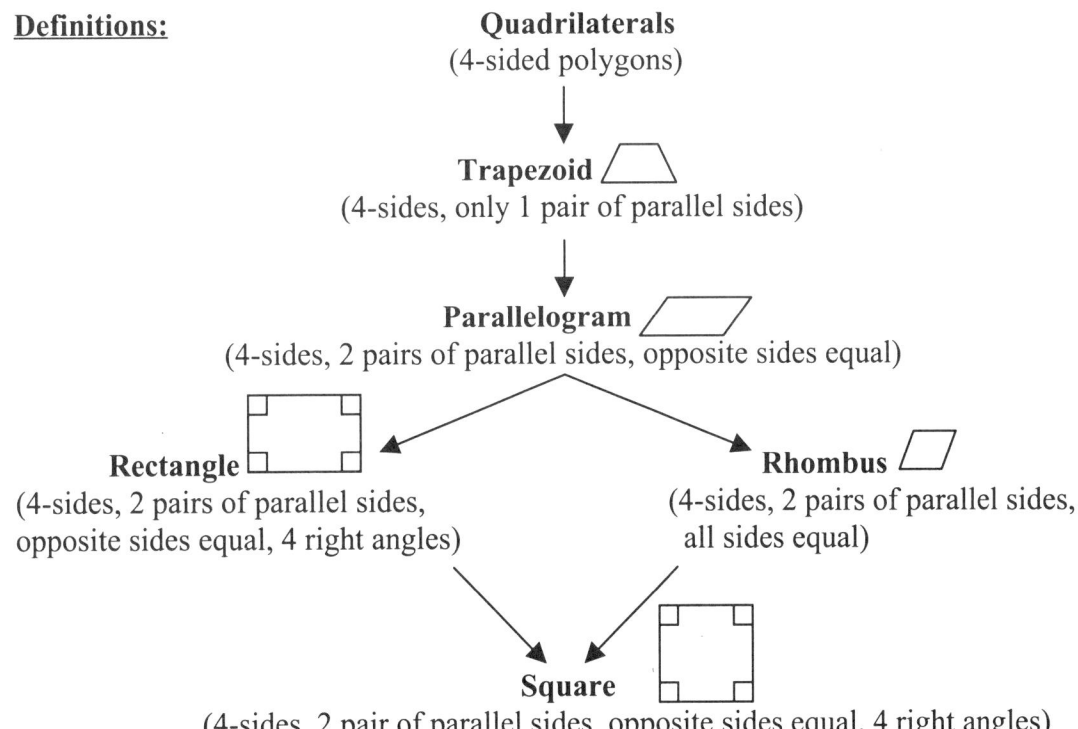

Identify the type of quadrilateral:

1. A quadrilateral with only one pair of parallel sides is called a(n) ?? .

   a. pentagon
   b. square
   c. parallelogram
   d. trapezoid

2. A quadrilateral with all sides equal and all angles equal is called a(n) ?? .

   a. pentagon
   b. square
   c. parallelogram
   d. trapezoid

3. A quadrilateral with all sides equal is called a(n) ?? .

   a. pentagon
   b. rhombus
   c. rectangle
   d. trapezoid

4. A quadrilateral with all right angles is called a(n) ?? .

   a. pentagon
   b. rhombus
   c. rectangle
   d. trapezoid

Parent Tip: The number of sides each has identifies the polygon. The first part of the word will tell you what kind of polygon it is. A pentagon has 5-sides (penta- means 5), hexagon has 6-sides (hexa- means 6), heptagon has 7-sides (hepta- means 7) and octagon has 8-sides (octa- means 8)

Identify the type of polygon:

5. Polygons with four sides are called ?? .

    a. triangles
    b. quadrilaterals
    c. pentagons
    d. hexagons

6. Polygons with five sides are called ?? .

    a. triangles
    b. quadrilaterals
    c. pentagons
    d. hexagons

7. Polygons with six sides are called ?? .

    a. pentagons
    b. hexagons
    c. heptagons
    d. octagons

8. Polygons with eight sides are called ?? .

    a. pentagons
    b. hexagons
    c. heptagons
    d. octagons

Definitions: Triangles
(3-sided polygon)

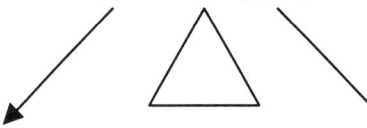

Classify by Sides
1. **Scalene Triangle** – no sides equal
2. **Isosceles Triangle** – with two equal sides
3. **Equilateral Triangle** – all sides equal

Classify by Angles
1. **Acute Triangle** – all angles are acute (less than 90°)
2. **Obtuse Triangle** – has an obtuse angle (greater than 90° and less than 180°)
3. **Right Triangle** – has a right angle (90°)

Classify the following triangles:

9. A triangle with a 90° angle is called a(n) ?? .

    a. acute triangle
    b. obtuse triangle
    c. right triangle

10. A triangle with all angles less than 90° is called a(n) ?? .

    a. acute triangle
    b. obtuse triangle
    c. right triangle

11. A triangle with an angle greater than 90° is called a(n) ?? .

    a. acute triangle
    b. obtuse triangle
    c. right triangle

12. A triangle with all sides the same measurements is called a(n) ?? .

    a. scalene triangle
    b. isosceles triangle
    c. equilateral triangle

13. A triangle with all sides different measurements is called a(n) ?? .

    a. scalene triangle
    b. isosceles triangle
    c. equilateral triangle

14. A triangle with only two sides the same measurement is called a(n) ?? .

    a. scalene triangle
    b. isosceles triangle
    c. equilateral triangle

Content Cluster: MEASUREMENT AND GEOMETRY

Objective: Students will identify angles and use properties of angles to solve problems for unknown angles.

> **Parent Tip:** The definitions of the different types of angles are based on their location to one another and their measurement.

Definitions:

Vertical Angles –
angles formed by two intersecting lines
that are across the vertex. The angles are equal.   ∠a = ∠b

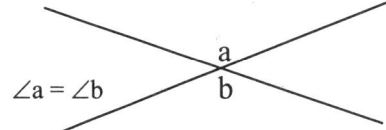

Adjacent Angles –
two angles that share the same vertex
and a common ray.   ∠c and ∠d
are adjacent angles.

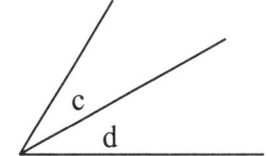

Complementary Angles –
two angles with measurements that add up to $90°$.

∠e and ∠f are complementary angles.

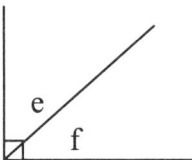

Supplementary Angles –
two angles with measurements that add up to $180°$

∠g and ∠h are complementary angles.

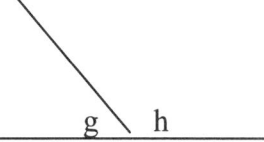

Use the following figure to answer questions 1-4:

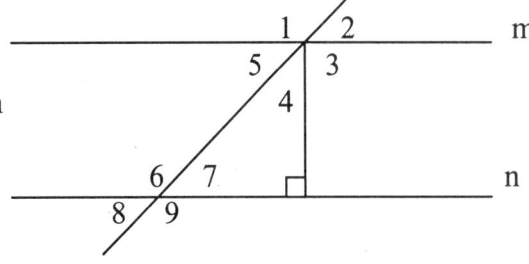

line m is parallel to line n

1. Which two angles are adjacent angles?

    a. ∠1 and ∠5   c. ∠6 and ∠9
    b. ∠2 and ∠5   d. ∠7 and ∠8

2. Which two angles are complementary angles?

    a. ∠1 and ∠5   c. ∠4 and ∠5
    b. ∠2 and ∠5   d. ∠4 and ∠3

3. Which two angles are supplementary angles?

   a. ∠1 and ∠3   c. ∠4 and ∠5
   b. ∠1 and ∠5   d. ∠4 and ∠3

4. Which two angles are vertical angles?

   a. ∠6 and ∠7   c. ∠9 and ∠7
   b. ∠6 and ∠9   d. ∠9 and ∠8

Use the following figure to answer questions 5-10:

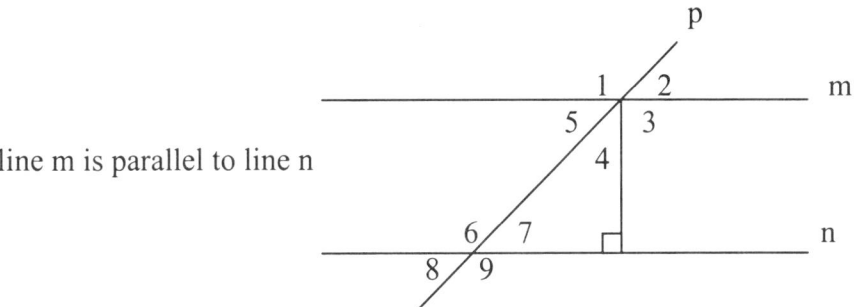

line m is parallel to line n

Find the measurement the angles: (*m*∠5 reads "the measure of angle 5")

5. If the *m*∠5 = 35°, what is the *m*∠2?

   a. 35°
   b. 45°
   c. 55°
   d. 65°

6. If the *m*∠4 = 45°, what is the *m*∠7?

   a. 35°
   b. 45°
   c. 55°
   d. 65°

7. If the *m*∠1 = 120°, what is the *m*∠2?

   a. 20°
   b. 40°
   c. 60°
   d. 80°

8. If the *m*∠8 = 115°, what is the *m*∠6?

   a. 55°
   b. 60°
   c. 65°
   d. 75°

9. If the *m*∠7 = 60°, what is the *m*∠4?

   a. 20°
   b. 30°
   c. 40°
   d. 50°

10. If the *m*∠2 = 40°, what is the *m*∠4?

    a. 50°
    b. 60°
    c. 70°
    d. 80°

Carney Educational Services How to Prepare for the CAT/6

Parent Tip: The sum of all three angles in a triangle is $180°$, so if you know two of the measurements of the angles you can solve for the third. In all parallelograms, rhombuses, rectangles and squares, the sum of all four angles is $360°$, opposite angles are equal and adjacent angles are supplementary.

Find the measurement of the angle:

11. What is the $m\angle B$ and $m\angle C$?

    a. 25°
    b. 35°
    c. 70°
    d. 80°

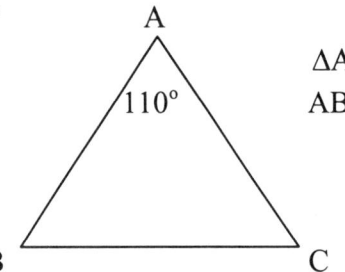

$\triangle ABC$ is an isosceles triangle.
$AB = AC$

Find the measurement of the angle:

12. What is the $m\angle G$?

    a. 53°
    b. 63°
    c. 143°
    d. 153°

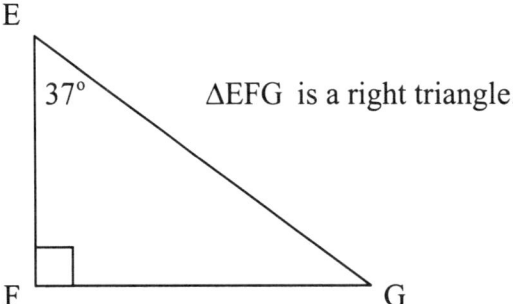

$\triangle EFG$ is a right triangle.

13. In parallelogram HIJK, if $m\angle J = 130°$, what is the $m\angle H$?

    a. 50°
    b. 90°
    c. 130°
    d. 150°

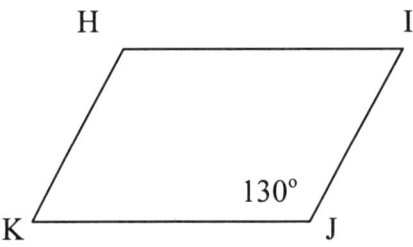

14. In rhombus LMNO, if $m\angle M = 75°$, what is the $m\angle L$?

    a. 75°
    b. 85°
    c. 95°
    d. 105°

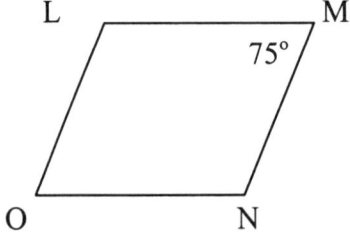

6th Grade Edition

Carney Educational Services — How to Prepare for the CAT/6

Content Cluster: STATISTICS, DATA ANALYSIS AND PROBABILITY

Objective: Students will compute and analyze statistical measurement for data sets.

> **Parent Tip:** The first thing that you do when working with data is **put the data in order** (least to greatest) if it isn't.

Definitions:

Range – the difference between the largest data and the smallest
Mean – the sum of all the data divide by the number of data
Median – the middle of the data
Mode – the most occurring data and there can be more than 1 mode in data

Example: (12, 18, 20, 12, 28, 22, 10) → put in order → (10, 12, 12, 18, 18, 22, 28)

Range → 28 – 10 = 18   Mean → $\frac{10 + 12 + 12 + 18 + 20 + 22 + 28}{7} = 17\frac{1}{7}$

Median → 18   Mode → 12 and 18

Use the set of data to answer questions 1-4:

(0, 1, 1, 2, 2, 2, 2, 3, 4, 5, 5, 6, 6)

1. Find the range.
   a. 3
   b. 4
   c. 5
   d. 6

2. Find the mean.
   a. 2
   b. 2.25
   c. 3
   d. 3.25

3. Find the median.
   a. 2
   b. 3
   c. 4
   d. 5

4. Find the mode.
   a. 1
   b. 2
   c. 5
   d. 6

Use the set of data to answer questions 5-8:

(3.6, 3.6, 1.4, 2.8, 2.4, 4.2, 3.3, 5.7)

5. Find the range.
   a. 4
   b. 4.2
   c. 4.3
   d. 5.7

6. Find the mean.
   a. 3.125
   b. 3.225
   c. 3.375
   d. 3.875

7. Find the median.
   a. 3.3
   b. 3.45
   c. 3.55
   d. 3.6

8. Find the mode.
   a. 2.8
   b. 3.3
   c. 4.2
   d. 3.6

Parent Tip: There are two terms that are used in the next section. **Outliers** – a part of the data that is much higher or lower than the rest of the data and **Central Tendency** – what is happening to the center of a set of data. The mean, median and mode are ways of locating the center.

Use the following set of data to answer questions 9-10:

(0, 0, 1, 1, 2, 3, 4, 20)

9. Which piece of data is the outlier?

   a. 1
   b. 2
   c. 3
   d. 20

10. How does the outlier effect the mean?

    a. decreases it
    b. increases it
    c. no effect on it

Use the following set of data to answer questions 11-12:

(1, 29, 30, 30, 31, 33)

11. Which piece of data is the outlier?

    a. 1
    b. 29
    c. 30
    d. 33

12. How does the outlier effect the mean?

    a. decreases it
    b. increases it
    c. no effect on it

Content Cluster: STATISTICS, DATA ANALYSIS AND PROBABILITY

Objective: Students will use data samples of a population and describe the characteristics and limitations of the sample.

> **Parent Tip:** There are two types of samples:
>
> **Representative Sample** – a sample selected from a population with the same characteristics as the target group.
>
> **Random Sample** – a sample where each selection has an equal chance of being included.

What type of sample:

1. You want to find out how many students like your school's cafeteria food. You survey 30 students entering the cafeteria for lunch.

   a. representative sample
   b. random sample

2. You want to find out how many students would like an after school sports program. You survey 50 students during recess.

   a. representative sample
   b. random sample

3. You want to find out how many girls in 5th grade want to start a jump rope club. You go to one of the three 5th grade classes and survey the girls.

   a. representative sample
   b. random sample

4. You want to find out the average hours spent on homework each day. You survey 50 students at lunch.

   a. representative sample
   b. random sample

> **Parent Tip:** Bias questions are unfair or lead you to a specific conclusion.

Fair and Biased Questions:

5. Do you prefer country or rock music?

    a. fair question   b. biased question

6. Do you like warm, comfortable, well-fitting shoes or stiff, hard boots?

    a. fair question   b. biased question

7. Do you prefer running a mile on a hot, humid day or sitting under a giant shade tree?

    a. fair question   b. biased question

8. Do you like the color red or blue better?

    a. fair question   b. biased question

9. Do you prefer cake or pie?

    a. fair question   b. biased question

10. Would you rather have a longer recess or a harder, longer, essay science test?

    a. fair question   b. biased question

Content Cluster: STATISTICS, DATA ANALYSIS AND PROBABILITY

Objective: Students will determine theoretical and experimental probabilities and use them to make predictions about events.

> **Parent Tip:** Probability is a <u>ratio</u> (fraction) where the numerator (top number) represents the <u>favorable</u> outcome (wanted results) and the denominator (bottom number) represents the <u>total</u> outcome (every possible result).
>
> Example: The probability of drawing a queen from a deck of cards → p (queen) = $\frac{4}{52} = \frac{1}{13}$
>
> The numerator 4 represents the number of queens in the deck (favorable outcomes).
> The denominator 52 represents the number of cards in the deck (total outcomes).

Use the following cards to answer questions 1-6:

3	3	1	2	7	3
4	7	5	6	1	4

If a card is picked from the cards above, find each probability:

1. p(3) =
   a. $\frac{1}{12}$
   b. $\frac{1}{3}$
   c. $\frac{1}{4}$
   d. $\frac{1}{6}$

2. p(6) =
   a. $\frac{3}{4}$
   b. $\frac{2}{3}$
   c. $\frac{1}{12}$
   d. $\frac{1}{6}$

3. p(1) =
   a. $\frac{1}{6}$
   b. $\frac{1}{4}$
   c. $\frac{2}{3}$
   d. $\frac{3}{4}$

4. p(3 or 4) =

a. $\dfrac{1}{4}$
b. $\dfrac{5}{12}$
c. $\dfrac{1}{6}$
d. $\dfrac{1}{12}$

5. p(4,5 or 6) =

a. $\dfrac{1}{6}$
b. $\dfrac{1}{4}$
c. $\dfrac{1}{2}$
d. $\dfrac{1}{3}$

6. p(1,2 or 3) =

a. $\dfrac{1}{2}$
b. $\dfrac{1}{4}$
c. $\dfrac{1}{3}$
d. $\dfrac{1}{6}$

A bag contains 3 orange marbles, 2 blue marbles, 5 yellow marbles and 4 red marbles.

Find each probability of getting the colored marbles:

7. p(orange) =

a. $\dfrac{1}{7}$
b. $\dfrac{3}{14}$
c. $\dfrac{5}{14}$
d. $\dfrac{2}{7}$

8. p(blue) =

a. $\dfrac{2}{7}$
b. $\dfrac{1}{7}$
c. $\dfrac{5}{14}$
d. $\dfrac{3}{14}$

9. p(yellow) =

a. $\dfrac{1}{7}$
b. $\dfrac{2}{7}$
c. $\dfrac{3}{14}$
d. $\dfrac{5}{14}$

10. p(blue or yellow) =

a. $\dfrac{1}{7}$
b. $\dfrac{2}{7}$
c. $\dfrac{1}{14}$
d. $\dfrac{1}{2}$

11. p(yellow or red) =

a. $\dfrac{1}{14}$
b. $\dfrac{3}{14}$
c. $\dfrac{5}{14}$
d. $\dfrac{9}{14}$

12. p(blue, yellow or red) =

a. $\dfrac{11}{14}$
b. $\dfrac{9}{14}$
c. $\dfrac{5}{14}$
d. $\dfrac{5}{7}$

Parent Tip: The probability of an outcome with two independent events, a coin and a die, multiply the probability of one event with the probability of the other.

Example: Using a die and a coin, what is the probability of heads on the coin and 3 dots on the die?

$$p(\text{heads}) = \frac{1}{2} \text{ and } p(3 \text{ dots}) = \frac{1}{6} \rightarrow p(\text{heads and 3 dots}) = \frac{1}{2} \times \frac{1}{6} = \frac{1}{12}$$

Suppose you flip 2 coins, find the probability:

13. p(heads and tails) =
    a. $\frac{3}{4}$
    b. $\frac{1}{2}$
    c. $\frac{1}{4}$
    d. 1

14. p(2 heads) =
    a. $\frac{3}{4}$
    b. $\frac{1}{2}$
    c. $\frac{1}{4}$
    d. 1

15. p(2 tails) =
    a. $\frac{3}{4}$
    b. $\frac{1}{2}$
    c. $\frac{1}{4}$
    d. 1

Suppose you roll a pair of dice, find the probability that the sum is:

16. p(8) =
    a. $\frac{5}{36}$
    b. $\frac{7}{36}$
    c. $\frac{1}{9}$
    d. $\frac{1}{12}$

17. p(10) =
    a. $\frac{5}{36}$
    b. $\frac{7}{36}$
    c. $\frac{1}{9}$
    d. $\frac{1}{12}$

18. p(2) =
    a. $\frac{1}{36}$
    b. $\frac{1}{24}$
    c. $\frac{1}{9}$
    d. $\frac{1}{12}$

> **Parent Tip:** When using an experimental probability, you base the probability on data you have collected and used that data to predict outcome.

You were asked to survey the students at your school to find out how they get home from school each day. You asked 50 students as they were leaving campus how they got home. 8 students walked home, 25 students carpooled, 10 students took the bus and 7 students rode their bikes. What is the probability that the next student asked:

19. will carpool?
    a. $\frac{1}{5}$
    b. $\frac{1}{2}$
    c. $\frac{7}{50}$
    d. $\frac{4}{25}$

20. will take the bus?
    a. $\frac{1}{5}$
    b. $\frac{1}{2}$
    c. $\frac{7}{50}$
    d. $\frac{4}{25}$

21. will walk?
    a. $\frac{1}{5}$
    b. $\frac{1}{2}$
    c. $\frac{7}{50}$
    d. $\frac{4}{25}$

Content Cluster: MATHEMATICAL REASONING

Objective: Students will make decisions about how to approach problems.

> **Parent Tips:** Many times word problems don't give you enough information to solve or too much information that can confuse the student but can still be solved. Make sure you read the problem carefully and the information can be used to solve the problem.

<u>Too Little or Too Much</u> - Read each of the following problems and decide if the information is too little (can't solve) or too much (but can solve).

1. At age 9, Stacy was 130 cm tall. She has a sister and two brothers. By the age of 14, she was 158 cm tall. How much had she grown in 5 years?

    a. Too Little   b. Too Much

2. Stella gets paid $12.00 per hour and overtime for every hour over 40 hours in a week. If she works 43 hours in 1 week, how much money did she make?

    a. Too Little   b. Too Much

3. Wilson has several pets. If he bought 3 more fish and sold one of his birds, how many pets does he now have?

    a. Too Little   b. Too Much

4. Maria has a stamp collection with 315 stamps. She bought a package of assorted stamps of the world. She gave half of the package to her friend. How large is her stamp collection now?

    a. Too Little   b. Too Much

5. A new car averages 20 miles to the gallon of gas. The owner has one week to test drive the car and is going on a 5 day, 1000-mile trip. If she leaves on a Tuesday and drives 7 hours a day, how many gallons of gas will she use?

    a. Too Little   b. Too Much

6. In Ms. Takes' class, $\frac{1}{4}$ of her class earned A', $\frac{1}{3}$ of her class earned B's and the rest of her class earned C's, D's and F's. How many students earned C's?

    a. Too Little   b. Too Much

Parent Tip: When solving a problem, you need to know what to do (mathematically) with the information. Sometimes you might have to add, then divide and finally multiply the number to get the answers. Ordering what to do is an important skill.

In the following problems, choose the best order to do the operations:

7. Jennifer earned, in the last 5 weeks, $18, $14, $20, $25 and $17. What was her weekly average earnings?

    a. add, then multiply
    b. multiply, then subtract
    c. add, then divide
    d. multiply, then divide

8. The area of a rectangle is 35 cm^2. The height of the rectangle is 7 cm. What is the perimeter of the rectangle?

    a. divide, then add
    b. multiply, then divide
    c. divide, then subtract
    d. subtract, then multiply

9. Henry went to the store and bought 5 items. They cost $1.49, $3.99, $2.25, $1.79 and $4.98. He gave the clerk a $20 bill. How much change did he get back?

    a. add, then divide
    b. multiply, then divide
    c. divide, then subtract
    d. add, then subtract

10. At the library book sale, paperback books were 3 for $1.00 and hardcover books were 2 for $3.00. What was the cost of 9 paperbacks and 6 hardcovers?

    a. subtract, then divide
    b. multiply, then add
    c. divide, then subtract
    d. multiply, then subtract

Content Cluster: MATHEMATICAL REASONING

Objective: Students will use strategies, skills and concepts in finding solutions.

> **Parent Tip:** Here are 6 strategies used in solving word problems:
> **Make a Table (chart)** – put your information in row and columns
> **Draw a Diagram** – pictures really help in solving problems
> **Work Backwards** – start with the end result, work toward the beginning
> **Logical Reasoning** – use common sense
> **Guess and Test** – try some numbers in the problem, see if they work
> **Look for a Pattern** – see if things are repeated

Choose the Best Strategy:

1. Waysville is 40 miles from Maysville. Staysville is 25 miles form Waysville. How far could Staysville be from Maysville?

    a. look for a pattern
    b. work backwards
    c. guess and test
    d. logical reasoning

2. Arman climbed a set of stairs and stopped at the middle step. From there, he walked down 3 steps, up 5 steps, down 4 steps and up 7 steps. He was at the top of the stairs, how many steps are in the set of stairs?

    a. look for a pattern
    b. work backwards
    c. draw a diagram
    d. make a table

3. Albert works at the student store after school. Nancy bought one $1.35 item. She gave Albert $2.00. How many ways could he make $0.65 in change without using pennies?

    a. look for a pattern
    b. work backwards
    c. draw a diagram
    d. make a table

4. What two integers have a sum of ⁻9 and a product of 45?

   a. guess and test
   b. make a table
   c. draw a diagram
   d. look for a pattern

5. It takes 4 minutes to make one cut through a board. How long will it take to cut a 12-ft. board into four equal pieces?

   a. guess and test
   b. make a table
   c. draw a diagram
   d. look for a pattern

6. Joseph and some friends are going to dinner and a movie. The movie starts at 8:00 PM. It will take 30 minutes to pick up his friends, 45 minutes to eat and they want to get to the theater 15 minutes before the movie. What time should Joseph leave his home?

   a. look for a pattern
   b. work backwards
   c. guess and test
   d. logical reasoning

MATH ANSWER KEY

Number Sense
(Computation Skills)
1. b
2. b
3. c
4. d
5. b
6. a
7. d
8. c
9. d
10. b
11. b
12. a
13. a
14. b
15. d
16. c
17. c
18. d
19. b
20. a
21. a
22. c
23. b
24. a
25. c
26. b
27. c
28. c
29. a
30. d
31. d
32. b
33. c
34. a
35. a
36. d
37. c
38. d
39. a
40. a
41. b
42. d
43. b
44. b
45. a
46. d
47. a
48. c
49. d
50. c
51. b
52. a
53. b
54. b
55. a
56. c
57. a
58. b
59. d
60. c
61. b
62. a
63. d
64. a
65. c
66. c
67. a
68. b
69. c
70. c
71. d
72. a
73. b
74. a
75. b
76. d
77. d
78. c
79. a
80. d
81. b
82. c
83. d
84. d

Number Sense
(Compare/Order Fractions)
1. c
2. a
3. c
4. b
5. c
6. a
7. c
8. a
9. b
10. c
11. a
12. b
13. a
14. b
15. a
16. c
17. c
18. a
19. d
20. c
21. d
22. d

Number Sense
(Fraction, Ratio, Proportions, Percent)
1. c
2. d
3. d
4. b
5. b
6. c
7. a
8. c
9. c
10. a
11. b
12. a
13. c
14. c
15. d
16. a
17. b
18. c
19. d
20. c
21. d
22. b

Number Sense
(Rational Numbers)
1. b
2. d
3. c
4. c
5. b
6. d
7. c
8. c
9. a
10. c
11. b
12. a
13. b
14. a
15. b
16. a
17. c
18. a
19. a
20. d

Algebra and Functions
(Verbal Expressions to Algebraic Expressions)
1. c
2. a
3. d
4. b
5. a
6. a
7. c
8. d
9. a
10. a
11. b
12. b
13. a
14. c
15. d
16. a
17. b
18. c

Algebra and Functions
(Evaluate Algebraic Expressions)
1. b
2. a
3. c
4. c
5. a
6. d
7. d
8. b
9. a
10. c
11. a
12. b

Algebra and Functions
(Solve Linear Equations)
1. c
2. b
3. b
4. a
5. d
6. c
7. d
8. c
9. a

10. b
11. c
12. b
13. b
14. d
15. a
16. a
17. c
18. c
19. a
20. c
21. c
22. b
23. b
24. d
25. a
26. d
27. c

Algebra and Functions
(Tables/Graphs)
1. c
2. d
3. d
4. a
5. b
6. c
7. b
8. c
9. a
10. c
11. b

Algebra and Functions
(Patterns)
1. b
2. c
3. a
4. c
5. d
6. c

Measurement and Geometry
(planes and solids)
1. d
2. b
3. c
4. a
5. b
6. b
7. a
8. b
9. c
10. a
11. c
12. d
13. d
14. d
15. a

Measurement and Geometry
(2-dimensional figures)
1. d
2. b
3. b
4. c
5. b
6. c

7. b
8. d
9. c
10. a
11. b
12. c
13. a
14. b

Measurement and Geometry
(Identifying Angles)
1. a
2. c
3. b
4. b
5. a
6. b
7. c
8. c
9. b
10. a
11. b
12. a
13. c
14. d

Statistics, Data Analysis, and Probability
(Mean, Median, Mode)
1. d
2. c
3. a
4. b

5. c
6. c
7. b
8. d
9. d
10. b
11. a
12. a

Statistics, Data Analysis, and Probability
(Samples)
1. a
2. b
3. a
4. b
5. a
6. b
7. b
8. a
9. a
10. b

Statistics, Data Analysis, and Probability
(Probability)
1. c
2. c
3. a
4. b
5. d
6. a
7. b
8. b
9. d

10. d
11. d
12. a
13. c
14. c
15. c
16. a
17. d
18. a
19. b
20. a
21. d

Math Reasoning
(Approach Problems)
1. b
2. a
3. a
4. a
5. b
6. a
7. c
8. a
9. d
10. b

Math Reasoning
(Strategies)
1. d
2. c
3. d
4. a
5. d
6. b

SOCIAL SCIENCE

WORLD HISTORY AND GEOGRAPHY: ANCIENT CIVILIZATIONS

Content Cluster: EARLY PHYSICAL AND CULTURAL DEVELOPMENT OF MANKIND FROM THE PALEOLITHIC ERA TO THE AGRICULTURAL REVOLUTION.

Objectives: To evaluate knowledge of: (1) the location and characteristics of the hunter-gatherer societies; (2) how humans adapted to a variety of environments; and (3) factors of the physical environment that gave rise to domestication of plants and animals and the increase in the sources of clothing and shelter.

> **Parent Tip:** Although factual knowledge is an essential element of the study of history and social science, analytical skills are key to the successful mastery of the subject. Help your child to view historical events in relation to each other, throughout time. Construct various timelines of key events, people, and periods of history. Make a special point to ask why events happened at a particular geographical location or time.

Choose the best answer.

1. Which of the following is <u>not</u> true of the Paleolithic Age?

    a. It was marked by the development of toolmaking about 2.5 million years ago.
    b. It is also known as the Old Stone Age.
    c. No artifacts remain from this era.
    d. Paleolithic people hunted wild animals and gathered wild plants for food.

2. _____, named by Louis and Mary Leakey, means "handy human."

    a. *Australopithecus*
    b. *Homo sapiens*
    c. *Homo habilis*
    d. Cro-Magnon

3. The important contribution of *Homo habilis* is

    a. scientists believe that they were the first toolmakers.
    b. they invented language.
    c. they were the first to use fire.
    d. they made very complex tools.

4. Various groups of *Australopithecines* lived

   a. after *Homo habilis*.
   b. before *Homo habilis*.
   c. after *Homo sapiens*.
   d. after *Homo erectus*.

5. *Homo erectus*

   a. learned to make fire.
   b. lived exclusively in Africa.
   c. had a smaller brain than *Homo habilis*.
   d. made more complex tools than Neanderthals.

6. *Homo sapiens* means

   a. "tool holder."
   b. "cave dweller."
   c. "safe one."
   d. "wise human."

7. Which of the following is <u>not</u> true of Neanderthals?

   a. The earliest fossils of *Homo sapiens* are called Neanderthal.
   b. Their fossils have been found in the Neander Valley in Germany.
   c. They are distinguished from *Homo erectus* by the size of their hands and eyes.
   d. They made more complex tools than *Homo erectus*.

8. Which of the following is <u>not</u> true of Cro-Magnon?

   a. Cro-Magnon lived before Homo erectus.
   b. Their fossils date from about 40,000 years ago.
   c. Cro-Magnon fossils have been found in France, Africa, and Asia.
   d. Cro-Magnon had a much larger brain than *Homo erectus*.

9. Cro-Magnons

   a. looked very different than people today.
   b. used the simplest tools of any hunter-gatherers.
   c. are believed to be the world's first artists.
   d. did not live in Europe.

10. During the Ice Age, _____ covered large areas of the earth, making it possible for human settlement to spread to different continents.

    a. land masses
    b. glaciers
    c. waterways
    d. trees

11. A glacier is a

    a. clear lake.
    b. mountain of snow.
    c. frozen river of ice.
    d. dessert of ice cream.

12. During the Ice Age, people adapted to the cold temperatures by

    a. burrowing in the snow.
    b. learning to make fire and sewing clothing from animal hides.
    c. growing facial hair.
    d. waiting for the climate to change.

13. Early toolmaking marked the dawn of

    a. carnivorous habits.
    b. cave drawings.
    c. deforestation.
    d. technology.

14. Culture can be defined as

    a. the topology, climate, and environment of a people.
    b. the beliefs of a people.
    c. the behaviors, beliefs, customs, and attitudes of a people.
    d. the language of a people.

15. Which of the following was not an advantage of using fire?

    a. roasting meat
    b. scaring away dangerous animals
    c. providing warmth
    d. building large camps

16. Which of the following factors did not contribute to the settling of hunter-gatherers?

    a. the development of storage bins for food
    b. plentiful game, wild grains, berries, plants, and roots in a particular location
    c. fresh water springs in a particular location
    d. the discovery of fences

17. Examples of domesticated plants and animals are:

    a. dogs, wolves, flowers, kernels
    b. sheep, goats, dogs, camels, wheat, corn, rice
    c. wild sheep, wild dogs, mountain goats, wild flowers
    d. shrubs, butterflies, deer, cows, pigs, fish

18. Another word for "agriculture" is

    a. food gathering
    b. domestication
    c. farming
    d. environment

19. Which of the following is not considered an advantage of agriculture over the hunter-gatherer lifestyle?

    a. People could live where there was little wild game and plants.
    b. Farmers and herders could raise more food than they could collect in the wild.
    c. Surplus food could be stored for another time or traded for other items.
    d. Farmers are less affected by the weather than hunter-gatherers.

20. An important result of the lifestyle shift to agriculture was that

    a. over time it led to the division of labor with people working at different kinds of jobs.
    b. it kept people from developing new skills.
    c. they developed less of a community spirit.
    d. people learned to build barns.

21. The term Neolithic Era

    a. comes from two Greek words, *neos* (new) and *lithos* (stone).
    b. comes from Greek mythology.
    c. comes from the Roman word for farmer.
    d. comes from the language spoken in the Neander Valley.

22. The beginning of the Neolithic Era was known for the following:

   a. People used stone tools, began to live in villages, made pottery for storing food and water, and wove cloth and baskets.
   b. People became less social with more idle time to spend by themselves.
   c. People refused to use stone tools because they were so heavy.
   d. The invention of sculpture and cave painting spread throughout Asia.

23. Toward the end of the Neolithic Era, people began to

   a. use stone tools.
   b. work with metals such as copper and bronze.
   c. migrate toward warm climates.
   d. lose control of their food supply.

24. Which of the following is <u>not</u> a true statement about Çatal Huyuk?

   a. It was a Neolithic trade center town located in what is now known as Turkey.
   b. The people of Çatal Hüyük did some hunting and gathering, as well as farming wheat, raising cattle, making stone tools, wooden bowls, reed baskets, and weaving cloth.
   c. Obsidian trading helped Çatal Hüyük to prosper.
   d. It had an extensive system of streets and roads.

25. The settlement of Umm Dabaghiyah in the Middle East

   a. had more houses than Çatal Hüyük.
   b. is believed to have been a hunting and trading outpost.
   c. was a self-sufficient town with fertile soil for farming.
   d. was famous for its clay pots.

26. Umm Dabaghiyah was

   a. located on the dry northern plain between the Tigris and Euphrates rivers.
   b. the hub of cattle trading in the Neolithic Era.
   c. the farming capital of the Middle East in the Neolithic Era.
   d. settled by people who refused to hunt animals for food.

Content Cluster: EARLY CIVILIZATIONS OF MESOPOTAMIA, EGYPT, AND KUSH.

Objective: To evaluate knowledge of the geographic, political, economic, religious, and social structures of these early civilizations.

Parent Tip: Discuss with your child the advances in agriculture and changes in society that occurred during this period in history. Focus on the factors that made the changes possible. Consider the special significance that geography played in the development of the human story. Refer to maps to help explain the relationships among various peoples throughout time.

Choose the best answer.

1. An irrigation system would include

    a. canals dug from riverbeds to fields.
    b. pulleys and chains.
    c. donkey or camel caravans.
    d. communication between neighboring farms.

2. Which characteristics best describe cities?

    a. large public buildings, leadership, self-sufficiency
    b. the ability to trade with other groups or settlements
    c. the existence of valuable resources
    d. large population with organization and leadership, different social groups, job and trade opportunities

3. The Ziggurat of Ur is an example of

    a. an irrigation canal.
    b. a golden musical instrument.
    c. a temple tower with a shrine at the top.
    d. a stone tablet unlocking the key to an ancient language.

4. Which of the following factors is <u>not</u> a result of surpluses?

    a. Surpluses lead to trade opportunities.
    b. People have a better chance of surviving famine and drought.
    c. People can specialize in certain types of work rather than only hunting and gathering food.
    d. Cities experience a decline in population.

5. Which of the following is <u>not</u> true?

   a. Hunter-gatherers are not considered a civilization.
   b. Civilizations are highly developed cultures that have distinctive architecture, music, religion, and laws.
   c. All cultures are considered civilizations.
   d. Social levels, specialization of labor, and a stable food supply are characteristics of civilizations.

6. Which of the following are examples of early civilizations?

   a. Ur and the Euphrates
   b. Nile Valley and the Fertile Crescent
   c. Tigris and Euphrates
   d. Çatal Hüyük and Umm Dabaghiyah

7. Mesopotamia means

   a. "the messy pot near the river."
   b. "the missed opportunity."
   c. "the land between the rivers."
   d. "the meandering rivers."

8. Which of the following is <u>not</u> true about the Mesopotamia?

   a. It includes all of present-day Iraq and parts of Turkey and Syria.
   b. The Tiger and Euripides rivers wind their way through the Mesopotamia.
   c. Irrigation was essential to the development of civilization in the Mesopotamia.
   d. The region called Sumer made up the southern part of the Mesopotamia near the Persian Gulf.

9. _____ ruled the city-states in the Mesopotamia region.

   a. Governors
   b. Kish
   c. Priests
   d. Merchants

10. The Sumerians

    a. developed a system of record-keeping to keep track of their trading.
    b. invented the game of bowling, called *bulla*.
    c. developed an irrigation system as a result of their trading.
    d. copied their neighbors' language and writing.

11. A _____ is a person who moves from place to place without settling down.

   a. scribe
   b. cuneiform
   c. nomad
   d. government administrator

12. Which of the following terms does not apply to writing?

   a. scribe
   b. cuneiform
   c. pictograph
   d. Kish

13. Which statement inaccurately describes the relationship between the religion and government in Mesopotamia?

   a. Priests ruled the early city-states, ran the irrigation systems, settled disputes, and collected taxes.
   b. Religion and government were combined.
   c. Surplus food was stored in the temples.
   d. Priests were only concerned with prayers, sacrifices, and the spread of religion. They were not a part of government.

14. The city-states of the Mesopotamian region eventually were conquered by

   a. Akkadian.
   b. Sargon.
   c. merchants.
   d. priests.

15. Hammurabi first came to power in _____, and would eventually rule all of Mesopotamia.

   a. Assyria
   b. Babylonia
   c. Akkad
   d. Egypt

16. Hammurabi's code

   a. was written on parchment so that it could be changed every month.
   b. gave the king the power to punish people for no reason.
   c. organized 282 laws that covered aspects of life that were important to his people.
   d. made no attempt to establish law and order or personal responsibility in the empire.

17. Which of the following is <u>not</u> true about the Nile River?

    a. Its regular flooding made farming impossible in Egypt.
    b. Papyrus reeds grew along its banks.
    c. It is the longest river in the world, flowing from central Africa to the Mediterranean Sea.
    d. It had cataracts of waterfalls and rapids.

18. The written history of ancient Egypt can be divided into three main periods when important events occurred:

    a. The Hieroglyphics period, the Golden Age, and the Iron Age.
    b. The Priests' Dynasty, the Kings' Age, and the Pharaohs' Period.
    c. The Idolatry Age, the Military Period, and the Royalty Age.
    d. The Old Kingdom period, the Middle Kingdom period, and the New Kingdom period.

19. Which of the following are important elements of the religion of the ancient Egyptians?

    a. They believed in one god, and they built the pyramids to please him.
    b. They believed in several gods whom they believed built the pyramids.
    c. They believed in several gods and looked forward to an afterlife.
    d. They believed that only privileged people would have an afterlife.

20. Regarding the relationship between religion and the social and political order in ancient Egypt,

    a. the priests owned all the land and controlled the government and the people.
    b. artisans and workers were in the highest levels of society.
    c. farmers were part of the highest social class in society.
    d. the upper social class included priests, tax collectors, and scribes.

21. Hatshepsut was a woman pharaoh known for

    a. building pyramids and expanding Egypt's borders.
    b. building obelisks, improving Egypt by restoring destroyed temples, and ruling during peace and propriety.
    c. being a great military leader.
    d. refusing to wear a false beard as a sign of being a ruler.

22. Ramses II, also known as Ramses the Great,

    a. had 10 children.
    b. ruled during a time when Egypt's military power was very weak.
    c. ruled for 67 years and built many large temples, including a huge one at Abu Simbel in Nubia.
    d. was a humble ruler who was not interested in honoring himself with monuments.

23. In the Old Kingdom period from about 2750 to 2260 B.C.

    a. most of the great pyramids were built.
    b. Egypt became a world power.
    c. the Nile River remained untamed.
    d. Upper Egypt and Lower Egypt had not yet united.

24. During the Middle Kingdom period from about 2061 to 1784 B.C.

    a. hieroglyphics were invented.
    b. most of the pyramids were built.
    c. Egypt became strong and achieved a great deal in architecture, art, and literature.
    d. scribes left Egypt to visit Assyria.

25. During the New Kingdom period from about 1570 to 1070 B.C.

    a. Egypt became powerful and prosperous by conquering other regions and expanding trade.
    b. Osiris, Anubis, Ra, and Amon became kings of Egypt.
    c. there was much confusion and disorder in Egyptian society.
    d. there were several weak leaders who came to power.

26. Which of the following statements is <u>not</u> true?

    a. Kush was located south of Egypt on the Nile River.
    b. After Hatshepsut died, Kush paid to Egypt annual "tribute" of ivory, oils, grains, and exotic animals.
    c. Kush was a kingdom rich in iron ore and wood, and its location helped it to become a trade center.
    d. The Nile River hindered the ability of Egypt and Kush to trade.

27. Which of the following does <u>not</u> describe the trade opportunities of the Kushites?

    a. Traders from the Middle East, Far East, and much of Africa arrived to trade for gold and ivory.
    b. There were no ports from which the Kushites could trade.
    c. Kushite merchants traded iron tools for glass and cloth from China and India.
    d. Kushite artisans, craftsmen, and jewelers sold their goods at Meroë.

28. Which of the following is <u>not</u> correct?

    a. The Sumerians are credited with inventing writing when they transformed pictographs into cuneiform.
    b. The cuneiform system had about 600 symbols and was used in the Middle East for about 2,000 years.
    c. The Phoenicians, who traded with people who used the cuneiform system, invented an alphabet with only 22 symbols.
    d. Hieroglyphics and cuneiform have been translated for thousands of years.

Content Cluster: EARLY CIVILIZATIONS OF THE ANCIENT HEBREWS

Objective: To evaluate knowledge of the geographic, political, economic, religious, and social structures of the Ancient Hebrews.

Parent Tip: Children understand history in a meaningful way when they are able to make connections between the past and their own lives. Discuss with your child the many contributions and traditions of the Ancient Hebrews that permeate the modern Western world.

Choose the best answer.

1. _____ was the first monotheistic religion based on the concept of one God who sets down moral laws for humanity.

    a. Canaan
    b. Judaism
    c. Torah
    d. Exodus

2. The story of the Israelites

    a. is found in the Torah, the first five books of the Hebrew Bible.
    b. tells of the development of the early settlers of what is now the country of Israel.
    c. is found in the Old Testament of the Christian Bible.
    d. all of the above.

3. Which of the following is <u>not</u> told in the Torah?

    a. God told Abraham, a shepherd from Mesopotamia, to go to Canaan.
    b. Abraham's descendants settled in Canaan and were called the Hebrews.
    c. The Hebrews became known as Israelites because Abraham's grandson, Jacob, changed his name to Israel.
    d. In Hebrew, Israel means "nomad who wanders with his flocks."

4. The Hebrews of Canaan

    a. remained there together for thousands of years in peaceful harmony with their neighbors.
    b. never experienced famine, because the land of Canaan was in the heart of a river delta.
    c. who left there to live in Egypt, became slaves in Egypt for over 400 years.
    d. had a series of strong leaders who tried to conquer Egypt and Assyria.

5. The Exodus was

   a. the journey of Moses and the Israelites from Egypt back to Canaan.
   b. the four hundred years that the Israelites spent being slaves in Egypt.
   c. the battle between Egypt and the Israelites led by Moses.
   d. the festival celebrated by the Israelites when they reached Egypt.

6. Which of the following are not among the common beliefs and teachings of Judaism and Christianity?

   a. A belief in one God who gave Moses the Ten Commandments on Mount Sinai.
   b. People can serve God by acting responsibly and righteously toward each other.
   c. The New Testament of the Bible, the Mishnah, and the Talmud.
   d. The idea that laws and justice should be fair and impartial to all people without regard to wealth.

7. Which of the following statements about King David of the Israelites is not true?

   a. He ruled the Israelites for forty years and helped them to defeat the Philistines.
   b. He captured the city of Jerusalem and declared it the capital of the Israelite nation.
   c. His son Solomon followed him to power.
   d. He was not the same David who, according to the Bible, faced Goliath with a slingshot.

8. After King Solomon's reign of peace and prosperity,

   a. the kingdom was split, such that the northern part with its capital of Samaria was called Israel, and the southern part with its capital of Jerusalem was called Judah.
   b. the Israelites became an even stronger world power.
   c. King Saul came into power and defeated the Assyrians and the Babylonians.
   d. the kingdom remained safe from military invasions.

9. The main Temple in Jerusalem

   a. was King Solomon's most famous building project.
   b. was a factor in keeping the Israelites united religiously despite being politically divided.
   c. was destroyed in 587 B.C. by the Babylonians along with the entire city of Jerusalem.
   d. all of the above.

10. After the Babylonians destroyed Jerusalem

    a. the prophets thought God had broken the covenant with the Jews.
    b. 15,000 Jews were exiled to Babylonia until Persia conquered Babylon.
    c. the Jews never rebuilt the great Temple.
    d. the Jews no longer believed in the covenant and rejected the teachings of the Torah.

11. Rabbi Yohanan ben Zaccai's compromise with the Romans when they invaded Palestine

    a. resulted in the Jewish religion being separated from Jewish political identity for the first time, thus enabling Judaism to become a world religion.
    b. allowed Jews to practice their religion while obeying Roman law.
    c. consisted of his agreement to accept Roman political rule if Rome allowed him to preserve Jewish tradition as a form of religious life.
    d. all of the above.

12. After the Romans destroyed Jerusalem's second Temple and expelled the Jews from Jerusalem and Palestine, the Jewish religion endured because

    a. the rabbis, who were Jewish teachers and community leaders, helped the Jews adapt.
    b. the Jews accepted the Torah as a central focus of Jewish life, more important than the place of worship.
    c. the Jews built synagogues wherever they lived so that they would have a place to worship, to study, and to gather socially.
    d. all of the above.

Content Cluster: EARLY CIVILIZATION OF THE ANCIENT GREEKS

Objective: To evaluate knowledge of the geographic, political, economic, religious, and social structures of the Ancient Greeks.

> **Parent Tip:** The study of the Ancient Greeks provides a wonderful opportunity to discuss forms of governments and various systems of rule. Discuss with your child the rights of citizens in the various city-states as they compare to the rights of citizens in America today. The contributions of the Greeks to philosophy, literature, art, and architecture are also of great significance. Help your child to recognize the lasting influence of the Ancient Greek culture on our modern lives.

Choose the best answer.

1. Which of the following terms are part of the geography of Greece?

    a. the Adriatic Sea, the Mediterranean Sea, Sardinia, rough rivers
    b. Peloponnesus, rugged mountains, islands in the Aegean Sea
    c. Asia Minor, Black Sea, Odysseus, Xenophon, clear lakes
    d. none of the above

2. Because of the unique geography of the region, the Ancient Greeks

    a. developed small, tightly knit communities, isolated from one another by mountains and sea inlets.
    b. made frequent trade contacts with Egypt, Phoenicia, Sicily, and Persia.
    c. grew grapes and olives to trade with other people for wheat, barley, and other grains.
    d. all of the above.

3. Homer's *Odyssey*

    a. was an epic poem based on oral poems and stories that were passed down during the 300 years of Greece's Dark Age.
    b. was a carved sculpture of a horse that appeared on the front of a sailing ship.
    c. was a trade ship that sailed to the Black Sea on a regular route.
    d. none of the above.

4. As the population of Greece grew,

    a. trade increased, and cities grew into large self-governing units called city-states.
    b. the people of Greece became increasingly isolated from each other and the rest of the world.
    c. the people of Greece concentrated on herding sheep and goats across the land.
    d. the nomadic way of life became the way of the future.

5. Ancient Greeks worshipped _____, whom they celebrated through myths and legends.

   a. Zeus, the master of the world, and his family of gods
   b. Homer and the *Iliad*, the military heroes of the day
   c. Coroebus, the first recorded winner of the Olympic games
   d. the ancient philosophers and thinkers of the day

6. Examples of the festivals held by the Ancient Greeks to honor their gods and goddesses were:

   a. the Festival of Dionysus, which combined religion, history and entertainment, in the form of plays such as the Greek tragedies and comedies.
   b. the sports competition at Olympia held to honor Zeus.
   c. the sports competition at Delos held to honor Apollo.
   d. all of the above.

7. Sanctuaries, the sacred sites where the Ancient Greeks honored and worshipped their gods,

   a. were private places not open to anyone outside of the region in which they were located.
   b. were modest, plain places where people went to bathe in the holy water.
   c. contained oracles, where priests and priestesses predicted events by interpreting messages from the gods.
   d. none of the above.

8. A(n) _____ is a form of government in which a small group of people rule.

   a. monarchy
   b. oligarchy
   c. dictatorship
   d. democracy

9. A(n) _____ is a form of government in which a king, queen, or emperor is the sole ruler.

   a. oligarchy
   b. bureaucracy
   c. monarchy
   d. democracy

10. A tyrant, in the context of Ancient Greece,

    a. was a leader who seized power by force, and ruled with total power.
    b. was sometimes cruel and harsh, yet was often sympathetic, reforming laws and helping the poor.
    c. taught the Greeks the value of uniting behind a leader to gain enough power to bring about change.
    d. all of the above.

11. The development of democracy began in the city-state of

    a. Sparta
    b. Athens
    c. Delphi
    d. Rhodes

12. Which of the following statements about the development of government is not accurate?

    a. Democracy arose out of a vacuum of power and a lack of leadership in a happy populace.
    b. The monarchy gave way to the oligarchy when nobles who helped the kings defend their land demanded to share in the king's power.
    c. The oligarchy was a step toward democracy because a group of nobles shared power equally with the king.
    d. Tyranny emerged from the people's discontent with the oligarchy's decisions, and democracy emerged from a more literate populace's discontent with overly harsh tyrants.

13. Which of the following was not a feature of the democracy of Athens?

    a. A council of 500 randomly chosen citizens met to propose new laws.
    b. An assembly of all the citizens of Athens met about every nine days to vote on the laws.
    c. Citizens served as jurors, regardless of wealth.
    d. All residents of the city-state, including women, foreigners, and slaves, were citizens who could participate in the democracy.

14. A major distinction between direct democracy and indirect democracy is

    a. in a direct democracy citizens vote on laws in an assembly.
    b. in an indirect democracy citizens elect officials to represent them in government.
    c. both "a" and "b"
    d. none of the above

15. The government of the city-state of Sparta

    a. evolved from a monarchy to an oligarchy, but never to a true democracy.
    b. had two kings who were part of a senate.
    c. had an assembly that elected 5 leaders called the ephors.
    d. all of the above.

16. Athens and Sparta

    a. had the same values and practices regarding education and military service.
    b. had such different values that they refused to join forces to defeat their common enemy.
    c. abolished slavery and the barter system within the walls of their city-states.
    d. none of the above.

17. Cyrus the Great, along with his son, Darius, and his grandson, Xerxes

    a. were from Greece and waged a war on Persia.
    b. were from Persia and waged wars on some of the city-states of Greece to extend the control of the Persian empire.
    c. were from Persia and pitted Athens and Sparta against one another, causing Greece to lose the Persian Wars.
    d. were from Persia and cared little about expanding their empire past the Aegean Sea.

18. During the Golden Age of Athens,

    a. Pericles, an elected leader, set military, political, and artistic goals for Athens.
    b. Sparta became a center of luxury, beautiful buildings, and education.
    c. there were no distinctions of social class, and slavery was abolished.
    d. all of the above.

19. If you went to Athens during the Golden Age, you would have seen

    a. beautiful public buildings and temples at the Acropolis on a hill in the middle of the city.
    b. the agora, or marketplace, below the Acropolis.
    c. the Parthenon, a marble temple built to honor the goddess Athena.
    d. all of the above.

20. Socrates and Plato

    a. were ancient Athenian philosophers and teachers who taught their students to question every aspect of their world and their lives.
    b. were bitter enemies who died when the plague came to Athens.
    c. were slaves who led a revolt in Sparta.
    d. were gods whom the Greeks worshipped at the sanctuaries at Delphi and Olympia.

21. The Peloponnesian War

    a. was over quickly because Athens' powerful navy joined forces with Sparta's strong army.
    b. was unaffected by the plague and the Persians giving money to Sparta.
    c. was fought between Athens and Sparta for twenty-seven years on land and sea.
    d. ended with Sparta surrendering to Athens in 404 B.C.

22. Macedonia was a large city-state just north of Mt. Olympus

    a. that became famous for being a peaceful kingdom that supported its neighbors.
    b. that became a military power under King Philip and his son Alexander.
    c. that never succeeded in conquering another region or country.
    d. none of the above.

23. Alexander the Great of Macedonia

    a. was an uneducated farmer who rose to power by rising through the cavalry ranks.
    b. despised the Greek culture and did everything in his power to destroy it.
    c. was a disciplined general and military genius who conquered Greece, Egypt, and the entire Persian empire in thirteen years.
    d. lacked vision and courage, was unambitious, unresourceful, lazy, and without ego.

24. Alexander the Great is associated with the Hellenistic Age

    a. which means "Greek-like" and represents the mixing of Greek and non-Greek Eastern cultures.
    b. because as he conquered lands, he spread knowledge of the Greek ways and left behind Greek rulers to influence and gain support of the conquered regions.
    c. because as he conquered lands, he adopted some of the ways of the conquered people in order to gain their support.
    d. all of the above.

25. Some of the contributions of the Greeks in the arts and sciences are:

    a. exquisitely carved sculptures based on Greek mythology; natural and lifelike figures that glorified the human body.
    b. epic poetry of Homer's the *Iliad* and the *Odyssey*; lyric poetry of Sapho about friendship and love.
    c. Herodotus, the father of history who wrote about the Persian Wars; Thucydides whose accounts of the Peloponnesian War used primary sources and eyewitness interviews.
    d. all of the above.

26. Among the contributions of the Greeks in the arts and sciences are:

    a. the Socratic method of teaching through the asking and answering of questions, as practiced by Socrates, Plato, and Aristotle.
    b. the use of the scientific method to investigate the cause of disease, as practiced by Hippocrates, often called the father of medicine.
    c. mathematicians Euclid's and Pythagoras' teaching and discoveries in the field of geometry.
    d. all of the above.

27. Words commonly used in present day English that refer to Ancient Greek culture include:

    a. spartan, referring to a simple, non-luxurious lifestyle.
    b. marathon, referring to a 25-mile run.
    c. tyrant, referring to a harsh ruler.
    d. all of the above.

Content Cluster: EARLY CIVILIZATIONS OF INDIA

Objective: To evaluate knowledge of the geographic, political, economic, religious, and social structures of Ancient India.

> **Parent Tip:** The achievements of Ancient India were enormous and long lasting. Discuss with your child some of the contributions of that civilization that permeate our world today, such as Aryabhata's discovery that the earth was a sphere that rotated around the sun, and that there were 365 days plus a few hours in the solar year. How was the world different before the invention of the Hindu-Arabic number system with its nine digits, zero, and the decimal? Two of the world's major religions, Hinduism and Buddhism, began in India and continue to guide the lives of hundreds of millions of people in our modern world. Analyze with your child how the doctrines of these belief systems compare with your own.

Choose the best answer.

1. Which of the following geographical features and physical events contributed to the development of India?

   a. The seasonal monsoon winds gave rise to rains followed by dry spells.
   b. The Himalyan and Hindu Kush mountain ranges gave rise to many river systems.
   c. the Indus River Valley and its fertile soil
   d. all of the above

2. The Indus Valley civilization

   a. existed from about 2700 B.C. to 1750 B.C.
   b. included 70 settlements, the largest being Mohenjo-Daro and Harappa.
   c. traded with Mesopotamia and Sumer.
   d. all of the above

3. Around 1500 B.C. the _____ migrated into India.

   a. Aryans
   b. Vedas
   c. monsoons
   d. none of the above

4. The Aryan contributions to Indian culture include:

   a. the Vedas, a collection of sacred hymns and poems.
   b. the caste system, identifying social subclasses.
   c. their spoken language, Sanskrit, the basis for the modern Hindi language.
   d. all of the above.

5. Which of the following was not an element of the social structure of the caste system?

   a. You could marry someone of a different caste from the caste to which you were born.
   b. The priests, or brahmans, were the most powerful class.
   c. The rulers called rajas and their warriors were in the second caste.
   d. The merchants and peasants were in the caste above the servants.

6. Vedism

   a. is also called Brahmanism because of the authority it gave to the Brahmans, or priests.
   b. was based on the Vedas, the hymns of the Aryans from about 1500 B.C.
   c. evolved into early Hinduism, which holds many of the same beliefs and continues to use the Vedas.
   d. all of the above

7. Hinduism, a major religion of present day India,

   a. presents a way of life through a vast variety of beliefs and practices, including many duties.
   b. suggests commitment to and respect for an ideal way of life, known as dharma.
   c. was passed down from generation to generation through the retelling of the epic poem, the *Mahabharata,* one section of which is the *Bhagavad Gita.*
   d. all of the above.

8. Sidhartha Gautama

   a. was a Brahman who spread the teachings of Hinduism and the Vedas.
   b. supported the rituals set forth in the Vedas and the practice of animal sacrifice.
   c. became known as the Buddha, or "enlightened one," who spread the dharma.
   d. was a warrior who urged the people of India to revolt against their rulers.

9. Which of the following was not part of the teachings of Buddha?

   a. People could find peace without the help of the priests' rituals.
   b. Animal sacrifices were important to show the gods respect and honor.
   c. People are equal and have the right to try to live a better life, a rejection of the caste system.
   d. The Four Noble Truths and the Eightfold Path can guide people through life and lead to enlightenment.

10. Which of the following beliefs is not a part of Buddhism?

    a. reincarnation
    b. karma
    c. excess
    d. nirvana

11. Buddhism spread through other cultures

    a. through missionaries sent outside of India by Asoka, an emperor who practiced Buddhism.
    b. as the conquering Mauryas expanded their empire throughout Asia.
    c. as the Mauryas followed established trade routes, teaching the dharma along the way.
    d. all of the above

12. The emperor Asoka, who ruled from 324 B.C. to 183 B.C.,

    a. left India to fight a series of wars that led to the fall of India.
    b. believed in nonviolence and that people should not harm humans or animals.
    c. resented his role as a ruler and treated his people harshly.
    d. none of the above

Content Cluster: EARLY CIVILIZATIONS OF CHINA

Objective: To evaluate knowledge of the geographic, political, economic, religious, and social structures of Ancient China.

> **Parent Tip:** The Chinese civilization is one of the oldest and most unique to survive to the present. Because its geography kept it somewhat isolated from other parts of the world, it presents an interesting context in which to apply the concepts of independent invention and cultural diffusion. Discuss the ways in which the past can be interpreted from different perspectives. Talk with your children about the various teachings of Confucius. What do they think about his ideas? Help them understand the enormity of the Silk Road in terms of its size and impact on the world's civilizations. What did silk fabric feel like to people who had always worn cotton and wool?

Choose the best answer.

1. The first civilization in Ancient China

   a. developed on the banks of the Chang Jiang, or Yangtze River.
   b. developed in the shadow of Mount Everest.
   c. developed on the banks of the Huang He, or "Yellow River,."
   d. developed on the shores of the Atlantic Ocean.

2. Which of the following geographical features contributed to China's isolation from the rest of the world and separated the cultural development of different regions within China?

   a. the Himalayas, the world's highest mountains
   b. the Gobi Desert, a dry wasteland
   c. other mountain ranges in the west and north
   d. all of the above

3. By about 5000 B.C., the Yangshao culture

   a. farmed where the Wei and the Hang He Rivers met.
   b. was settled by seafaring people who lived in grass huts.
   c. traded with Mesopotamia and Sumer.
   d. none of the above

4. By about 3000 B.C., the Lungshan culture

   a. used simple written symbols and numbers.
   b. produced pottery with a potter's wheel and kiln, and harvested silk from silkworms to weave fabrics.
   c. farmed using irrigation and flood control techniques, hunted, fished, raised domesticated animals, and eventually grew rice.
   d. all of the above

5. The Yangshao and Lungshan cultures

   a. disappeared forever without an archaeological trace.
   b. are revealed in the written histories of Xia.
   c. laid the foundations for the first true Chinese civilization, the Shang dynasty.
   d. were greatly influenced by their proximity to the Himalayas.

6. A dynasty is

   a. the spouse of the king or queen.
   b. a series of rulers from the same family.
   c. found only in Chinese history.
   d. the set of laws for inheriting property.

7. Among the lasting contributions of the Shang dynasty was

   a. mixing tin and copper to produce bronze.
   b. ancestor worship.
   c. the earliest known Chinese writing.
   d. all of the above.

8. Confucius, who lived from 551 B.C. to 479 B.C.,

   a. refused to study and awaited his time to inherit the kingdom of his family.
   b. started a new religion in China during a time of peace, stability and calm among a satisfied people.
   c. became a teacher of a code of behavior and ethical system that is described in the Analects.
   d. lived during a time when few people questioned their lives and times or their culture's rules and values.

9. Which of the following are not among the teachings of Confucianism?

   a. The foundation of all relationships, from family to government, should be sincerity, loyalty, and mutual respect.
   b. Children may never disagree with their parents.
   c. Children may disagree with their parents, but they should remain reverent and obedient.
   d. Government should rule by good example, not with harsh laws and punishment.

10. At the same time Confucianism was being taught, another movement called Taoism

    a. stressed Jen, the concept of one person being in harmony with another.
    b. stressed the importance of the rule of law above everything else.
    c. stressed universal love for everything and everyone.
    d. stressed becoming one with the natural flow of nature and all things in the universe.

11. Qin Shihuangdi

    a. conquered and unified the warring states of China into one empire.
    b. was the last emperor of China.
    c. wanted to be called king.
    d. rose to power through peaceful discussion with the people.

12. Which of the following were not among the contributions of Qin Shihuangdi?

    a. He ended feudalism, and established provinces and districts with an administrative system of workers.
    b. He unified money, weights and measures, and the writing system that could be used in China.
    c. He built the Great Wall of China to keep Chinese nomads in and to keep enemies out.
    d. He encouraged people to read everything and write books on all subjects.

13. After the death of Qin Shihuangdi, the Han dynasty rose to power and ruled from 206 B.C. to 220 A.D. During this time,

    a. the principles of Confucianism were made part of the laws.
    b. China was a land of peace, prosperity, exploration, and invention.
    c. the Han Chinese invented acupuncture, mining for salt, the seismograph, paper, and the first Chinese dictionary.
    d. all of the above

14. During the Han dynasty,

    a. there was little interest in what was happening in the West.
    b. China started colonies in North Korea and North Vietnam, and conquered the people of the Gobi Desert.
    c. Chinese explorers reported that there was no wealth or civilization outside of China.
    d. China suffered from internal strife and chaos that prevented it from growing.

15. The Silk Road

    a. was a well-known trade route that linked China with the Middle East and Rome.
    b. allowed China to trade silk for things from the West, such as horses, grapes, and alfalfa.
    c. resulted in Buddhism being spread from India to China.
    d. all of the above.

Content Cluster: THE DEVELOPMENT OF THE ROMAN EMPIRE

Objective: To evaluate knowledge of the geographic, political, economic, religious, and social structures in the development of Rome.

Parent Tip: Continue developing a timeline of history with your child so that he or she can better understand the flow of history and link important events to a time frame. It is important to keep a map handy, to help build an understanding of the geography of the regions and the relationships among the emerging and declining empires.

Choose the best answer.

1. Early Latin legends recount stories of

    a. a wolf that rescues two orphan twins, descended from Aeneas of Troy, who were floating down the Tiber River.
    b. Romulus and Remus, two sisters who built the city of Rome and ruled jointly in peace.
    c. how Remus built the city of Rome.
    d. how the gods built Rome in a deep canyon.

2. Rome's history can be divided into three major periods. Which one of the following is not one of them?

    a. the Latin Vatican period from 1000 B.C. to 600 B.C.
    b. the rule of the kings until 509 B.C.
    c. the period of the republic from 509 B.C. to 31 B.C.
    d. the Roman empire, which survived until 476 A.D.

3. Which of the following geographical factors did not influence the development of Rome?

    a. It was part of a large plain where people could herd and farm.
    b. The monsoon winds brought constant rains and floods.
    c. Its seven hills provided a place for protective forts and its river made trade easier.
    d. It was located on a peninsula that extended into the Mediterranean Sea, which helped it to trade with Greece, Spain, Egypt, and the rest of North Africa.

4. Following the overthrowing of King Tarquin the Proud in 509 B.C., Rome established

    a. a plebiscite, with a citizens' advisory group.
    b. a democracy, where everyone had equal economic and political power.
    c. a republic, where citizens elected representatives to run the government, and there was no monarch.
    d. a monarchy, where citizens ruled with enough power to advise the king.

5. In the early form of the new government,

   a. all citizens could vote, but only some of them were allowed to hold office.
   b. the Senate advised the consuls.
   c. a citizen assembly elected leaders, called consuls.
   d. all of the above

6. There were two classes of citizens in the republic, the patricians and the plebeians, both determined by birth. Which of the following is true?

   a. The plebeians were the elite class, usually inherited nobility.
   b. The patricians were rich, and could hold religious, political, or military office.
   c. Only the plebeians could vote and be members of the Senate.
   d. The patricians outnumbered the plebeians, but the plebeians held all of the power.

7. In addition to the distinctions between the patricians and the plebeians, which of the following existed in the early republic?

   a. A division existed between citizens and slaves.
   b. A poor person who borrowed money from another became that person's slave through debt bondage.
   c. Women could not vote, own property, or participate in government, but were protected by laws.
   d. All of the above

8. When the plebeians demanded change by withdrawing from Rome, which of the following did not occur?

   a. They formed their own assembly and elected their own officials called tribunes.
   b. They published the Roman laws on twelve bronze tablets for all to see.
   c. They could not abolish debt bondage, no matter how hard they tried.
   d. They won the right for laws passed by the plebeian assembly to apply to patricians, too.

9. Which of the following characteristics of the American government began in Rome?

   a. checks and balances, so that one branch of government can not overpower another one
   b. the veto power, which cancels legislative action
   c. a balanced tripartite government (three groups with different responsibilities) and a written constitution
   d. all of the above

10. An important way that Rome expanded its territory was

    a. by making allies of other countries and sharing its wealth with them in exchnge for their allegiance in war.
    b. by starving and punishing everyone who resisted Rome, and denying them citizenship.
    c. by sending its teachers and missionaries to persuade others to join its peaceful quest.
    d. by never losing a battle or a war on land or sea.

11. Carthage

    a. remained the major Mediterranean power throughout Rome's existence.
    b. was a region of North Africa that fought with Rome over control of Sicily, Spain, and the Mediterranean area.
    c. was a part of Phoenicia that joined forces with Rome to defeat Hannibal in the Punic Wars.
    d. was an ally of Rome at the time of Hannibal's rule.

12. As a result of Rome's expansion,

    a. it eventually controlled Italy, most of Western Europe, Macedonia, Greece, Spain, Gaul, Asia Minor, and North Africa.
    b. the rich citizens of Rome had grown richer, but there were more unhappy, poor people and slaves.
    c. the generals in the Roman army were competing with each other for power and there were civil wars.
    d. all of the above

13. The Roman republic system of government ended in about 46 B.C.

    a. when Julius Caesar defeated Pompey and declared himself dictator for life.
    b. when Hannibal defeated Caesar on Roman soil.
    c. when the slaves won a rebellion led by Sparticus.
    d. when Rome went bankrupt after the generals looted the treasury.

14. During the rule of Julius Caesar,

    a. few public buildings or temples were constructed.
    b. Caesar stayed at home in Rome, cared little about the rest of the world, and refused to meet foreign leaders.
    c. some Senators disliked his arrogant attitude and suspected that he wanted to usurp their power, make himself king, and start a dynasty.
    d. most citizens resented the changes he made, such as higher taxes and taking away farmland.

15. *"Et tu, Brute?"* refers to

   a. Caesar's last words, spoken to his friend, Brutus, as he assassinated Caesar in the Senate.
   b. the moment when Caesar turned the keys of government over to his son, Brutus.
   c. the brutish weather on the Ides of March, the day when Caesar was crowned king.
   d. words of praise from the people of Rome to Brutus after Caesar's assassination.

16. Which of the following statements is incorrect?
   a. After Caesar's death, his son Octavian came into power.
   b. Octavian and Caesar Augustus are different people.
   c. Octavian's rule began the peaceful period called *"Pax Romana"* when Rome had no rivals with sufficient power to threaten its dominance.
   d. Within the city of Rome, Augustus fed the hungry, built beautiful temples and buildings, and established police and fire departments.

17. Augustus

   a. forbade the people to participate in the arts.
   b. was a weak leaders who did not care about government or its organization.
   c. claimed to be restoring the republic system of government, but is considered by historians to have ruled as an emperor.
   d. abandoned the reforms begun by his father and failed to recognize the problems of Rome.

18. Which of the following is not true of *Pax Romana?*

   a. It refers to 200 years of peace and prosperity in Rome as the Roman Empire expanded all the way to Britain, Africa, and Asia.
   b. During this period, cities in Roman provinces around the world were built like Rome with public baths, temples, and amphitheaters.
   c. It brought change to the world through the spread of the Roman ideas, customs, language, and religion.
   d. In the provinces people were not allowed to become Roman citizens, to participate in government, to conduct business in Rome, or to own property, so they constantly rebelled.

19. The Roman economy

   a. was driven in large measure by its need to acquire grains to feed its enormous professional army and its poor city dwellers.
   b. was affected by the huge number of its farmers who could not make a profit, save money, or afford to buy luxuries.
   c. depended on Mediterranean shipping routes to market gold and silver from Spain, lead and tin from Britain, silks from the East, and to obtain grain from Spain, Egypt, and North Africa.
   d. all of the above

20. Regarding the religion that was an integral part of the Roman state:

    a. It was similar to the religion of the ancient Greeks, because the Romans worshipped many gods whom they believed controlled every aspect of their lives.
    b. It was not so much a philosophy that gave people ideas to live by, but centered on rituals and omens that involved animal sacrifice.
    c. Because it did not contain an ethical framework that suggested how people ought to act, Romans began to show interest in other religions.
    d. All of the above

21. Much of what we know about the early history of the Christians comes from the New Testament of the Christian Bible

    a. which tells the story of Jesus, a Jew from Nazareth, and his followers.
    b. which tells the story of a Roman citizen who was a Jew known as Saul or Paul, who changed from criticizing Christians to spreading Christian beliefs throughout the Roman empire.
    c. which tells that Jesus was raised as a Jew, studied the Torah, and became a religious teacher.
    d. all of the above

22. Which of the following beliefs did Jesus not teach?

    a. the traditional Jewish teachings of one God, the Ten Commandments and the words of the Jewish prophets
    b. Treat your friends with kindness and love, ignore the poor, and punish your enemies with great harshness and cruelty, because the Roman gods will not favor anything else.
    c. The coming of the kingdom of God was near.
    d. All of the above

23. Although the Jews and early Christians lived in the same communities and shared many common beliefs,

    a. the Jews believed that the messiah referred to by the prophets had not yet come, but when he did he would overthrow the Roman government and reunite the Jews.
    b. the Christians believed that Jesus was the messiah who would not free the Jews from Roman rule, but would bring eternal life.
    c. they disagreed about the extent that people had to follow Jewish law, which eventually resulted in the formation of two separate religions.
    d. all of the above.

24. Saul, known to Christians as St. Paul the Apostle,

    a. spread the teachings of Christianity as he traveled throughout the Roman Empire.
    b. never accomplished his goal of starting new Christian communities.
    c. believed that the laws of Judaism were more important than belief in Jesus.
    d. urged people to disobey the Roman laws.

25. By 64 A.D., distrust of the Christians had grown in Rome

    a. because they did not worship the Roman gods or participate in their festivals.
    b. because Emperor Nero had blamed them for the burning of the city of Rome.
    c. because they did not share many Romans' attitudes about acquiring wealth and property.
    d. all of the above

26. The Romans' persecution of the Christians ended

    a. when Constantine became emperor and promoted Christianity throughout the empire.
    b. and the church became more powerful.
    c. all of the above
    d. none of the above

27. Which of the following are not among the enduring contributions of the Romans?

    a. 50,000 miles of roads that promoted trade and communication throughout the world, many of which are still in use today
    b. The invention of concrete, the perfection of the arch in architecture, and surveying
    c. The concept of a non-paid volunteer army without organization, training, or support
    d. A legal system with courts, judges, and lawyers.

SOCIAL SCIENCE ANSWER KEY

Paleolithic Era to the Agricultural Revolution
1. c
2. c
3. a
4. b
5. a
6. d
7. c
8. a
9. c
10. b
11. c
12. b
13. d
14. c
15. d
16. d
17. b
18. c
19. d
20. a
21. a
22. a
23. b
24. d
25. b
26. a

Mesopotamia, Egypt, and Kush
1. a
2. d
3. c
4. d
5. c
6. b
7. c
8. b
9. c
10. a
11. c
12. d
13. d
14. b
15. c
16. c
17. a
18. d
19. c
20. d
21. b
22. c
23. a
24. c
25. a
26. d
27. b
28. d

Ancient Hebrews
1. b
2. d
3. d
4. c
5. a
6. c
7. d
8. a
9. d
10. b
11. d
12. d

Ancient Greece
1. b
2. d
3. a
4. a
5. a
6. d
7. c
8. b
9. c
10. d
11. b
12. a
13. d
14. c
15. d
16. d
17. b
18. a
19. d
20. a
21. c
22. b
23. c
24. d
25. d
26. d
27. d

Ancient India
1. d
2. d
3. a
4. d
5. a
6. d
7. d
8. c
9. b
10. c
11. d
12. b

Ancient China
1. c
2. d
3. a
4. d
5. c
6. b
7. d
8. c
9. b
10. d

11. a
12. d
13. d
14. b
15. d

Ancient Rome
1. a
2. a
3. b
4. c
5. d
6. b
7. d
8. c
9. d
10. a
11. b
12. d
13. a
14. c
15. a
16. b
17. c
18. d
19. d
20. d
21. d
22. b
23. d
24. a
25. d
26. c
27. c

VOCABULARY RELATED TO SOCIAL STUDIES CONTENT CLUSTERS

> **Parent Tip:** The words on this list appear in the exercises of this book within the content clusters noted, but are not specifically tested. (Many words that are essential to the understanding of a content cluster, such as *Neolithic* or *irrigation,* are tested in the exercises themselves.) The words listed below are likely to recur quite often in your child's history/social science text. Make sure he or she can formulate sentences using these words. You will find that they will serve as an excellent springboard for discussion on a variety of subjects.

EARLY CULTURAL DEVELOPMENT OF MANKIND

artifact
exclusively
fossils
distinguished from
complex
agriculture
topology
domesticated

technology
surplus
lifestyle
self-sufficient
fertile
era
mythology

EARLY CIVILIZATIONS OF MESOPOTAMIA, EGYPT, AND KUSH

outpost
hub
shrine
famine
drought
decline
culture
civilization
specialization
stable
nomad
scribe
pictograph
cuneiform
inaccurate
dispute
merchant
code
parchment
cataract
hieroglyphics

dynasty
idolatry
kingdom
afterlife
artisan
kiln
pharaoh
obelisk
restore
temple
prosperous, prosperity
humble
monument
architecture
disorder
exotic
transform

EARLY CIVILIZATIONS OF THE ANCIENT HEBREWS

monotheistic
moral, ethical
descendants
harmony
delta
common
defeat
invasion
despite
prophet

covenant
exile
reject
compromise
identity
enabling
preserve
endure
adapt
synagogue

EARLY CIVILIZATIONS OF THE ANCIENT GREEKS

isolated, isolation
inlet
epic
oracle
interpret
monarchy
oligarchy
dictatorship
democracy
oligarchy
bureaucracy
tyranny, tyrant
vacuum
populace
discontent
randomly
resident

citizen
evolve
assembly
ephor
abolish
barter
slavery
wage war
agora
philosopher, philosophy
plague
despise
Hellenistic
exquisite
primary source
spartan

EARLY CIVILIZATIONS OF INDIA

monsoon
fertile
sacred
caste
Vedas, Vedism
dharma
ritual
enlightened

sacrifice
reincarnation
karma
excess
nirvana
missionary
nonviolence

EARLY CIVILIZATIONS OF CHINA

seafaring
ancestor
proximity
spouse
inherit
stable, stability
reverent

harmony
universal
feudalism
dynasty
acupuncture
seismograph

DEVELOPMENT OF THE ROMAN EMPIRE

strife
chaos
patrician
plebeian
elite
nobility
veto
tripartite
ally, allies
looted
usurp
arrogant
rival
dominant, dominance
republic
emperor
province
acquire
professional
Old Testament
New Testament
Torah

SCIENCE

Content Cluster: PLATE TECTONICS AND EARTH'S STRUCTURE

Objective: To evaluate knowledge of plate tectonics and how this subject is involved in the major geologic events and surface features of the Earth.

> Parent Tip: To help your child understand the idea of plate tectonics one must explain that the earth is made of layers. Several layers of different material cover the inner core. The solid top layer is made of individual plates that are continually moving. They can collide to form landmasses such as mountains, move over hot spots to form volcanoes, and slip when they are in direct contact with each other to cause earthquakes.

Choose the correct answer:

1. Which of the following is part of the theory of tectonics?

    a. The earth's outer shell is made of many plates that are continually moving and coming into contact with each other.
    b. The earth's outer shell is made of one solid plate that is continually growing but not moving.
    c. The earth's outer shell is made of many plates, which over time will join into one large plate.
    d. The earth's outer shell is made of one solid plate that is continually shrinking.

2. Which of the following provide evidence for the theory of plate tectonics?

    a. the distribution of fossils on various continents
    b. similar rock formations and mountain ranges on various continents
    c. the way the continents seem to fit together
    d. all of the above

3. In ancient times, the single land mass that is thought to contain all of the continents was called

    a. Asia Minor.
    b. Eurasia.
    c. Pangaea.
    d. Ameriasia.

4. The most common cause of earthquakes is

    a. wind movement.
    b. water movement.
    c. oil drilling.
    d. plate movement.

5. The uppermost rigid and solid layer of the earth is known as the

    a. atmosphere.
    b. lithosphere.
    c. hemisphere.
    d. hydrosphere.

6. In plate tectonics, the areas where the plates are moving apart are called

    a. convergent boundaries.
    b. transformed boundaries.
    c. divergent boundaries.
    d. strike-slip boundaries.

7. The three main layers of the earth (from the deepest to the surface layer) are called

    a. the core, the mantle, and the lithosphere.
    b. the mantle, the core, and the lithosphere.
    c. the lithosphere, the mantle, and the core.
    d. the lithosphere, the core, and the mantle.

8. When an oceanic plate continually pushes up on a continental plate, or when two continental plates collide, which of the following will probably happen?

    a. A new ocean will be formed.
    b. A mountain range will be formed.
    c. More trees will be created.
    d. The land will become more fertile.

9. The movement of the continental land masses away from each other is called

    a. the continental divide.
    b. the continental drift.
    c. the continental erosion.
    d. the continental migration.

10. Breaks in land masses where hot magma reaches the surface is an example of

    a. a canyon.
    b. a volcano.
    c. an earthquake.
    d. a glacier.

11. A break in the earth's crust that can move up, down, or sideways is called a

    a. fault
    b. plateau
    c. pore
    d. current

12. How fast do the tectonic plates move?

    a. Several miles per year.
    b. Several kilometers per year.
    c. Several centimeters or inches per year.
    d. Only a few centimeters every hundred years.

13. When a weak spot in the earth's crust moves over a hot spot in the mantle, what generally happens?

    a. An earthquake.
    b. A volcano or fissure forms.
    c. An island becomes more tropical.
    d. The crust passes over undisturbed.

14. Which of the following answers can have influence on the effect of an earthquake?

    a. The magnitude of the quake.
    b. The distance from the epicenter.
    c. The composition of the land mass.
    d. All of the above.

15. Hot molten rock that is found deep under the earth's crust is called

    a. magma
    b. lava
    c. ash
    d. cinder

Content Cluster: SHAPING THE EARTH'S SURFACE

Objective: To evaluate knowledge of the effect of weathering and erosion on the topography of the Earth's land masses.

> **Parent Tip:** The study of topography includes the physical features of the Earth's surface. The main agents of erosion that reshape the landscape are water, wind, ice, plants, and gravity. Natural hazards such as earthquakes, volcanoes, landslides, and floods change the topography, destroy habitats, and harm animal and plant life.

1. The process of breaking down rocks and other materials by wind, water, and ice is called

    a. weathering.
    b. uplifting.
    c. sedimentation.
    d. crystallization.

2. One of the problems of water erosion of soils is

    a. the fertile topsoil is washed away.
    b. the nutrients and minerals in the ground are washed away.
    c. the ground becomes unstable and can have land slides.
    d. all of these

3. The process of building new landforms by laying down sediments is called

    a. leaching.
    b. decomposition.
    c. oxidation.
    d. deposition.

4. Glaciers are

    a. fast moving rivers that cause erosion.
    b. large masses of moving ice and snow that cause erosion.
    c. fast moving wind storms that cause erosion.
    d. powerful waves that cause erosion.

5. Which factor has the greatest effect on the shape of the shoreline?

    a. the wind
    b. the rivers entering the ocean
    c. the pounding of the ocean waves
    d. the freezing of the water in winter

6. The area where a river flows into a lake or ocean is called a

    a. levee.
    b. delta.
    c. sand bar.
    d. flood plain.

7. As waves erode the cliffs of rock near the sea, some of the rock is left in columns called

    a. terraces.
    b. sea stacks.
    c. salt pillars.
    d. moraines.

8. Rock and other debris that is deposited by glaciers is called

    a. dune.
    b. till.
    c. humus.
    d. loess.

9. Volcanoes

    a. destroy plant and animal life
    b. can cause an island to form over time
    c. cause erosion of the soil
    d. all of the above

10. Weathering of rock caused by solid particles hitting or rubbing against them is

    a. abrasion.
    b. oxidation.
    c. deposition.
    d. sedimentation.

11. Small moving branches of water that eventually flow into larger rivers are called

    a. veins.
    b. meanders.
    c. tributaries.
    d. arteries.

Content Cluster: THERMAL ENERGY

Objective: To evaluate knowledge of how heat moves from warmer objects to cooler objects through various processes.

> **Parent Tip:** Energy is the ability to do work. It is never destroyed but it changes from one form to another. Heat flow, waves of light, water, or sound can carry energy from one place to another. Heat energy causes changes in temperature and in the phase (solid, liquid, gas) of any form of matter. It can be passed on to other objects in several ways.

1. When heat moves through a material without the material moving itself (metal spoon in hot water), the process is called

    a. radiation.
    b. convection.
    c. conduction.
    d. absorption.

2. When heat moves through a material by actual movement of the material (boiling water), the process is called

    a. radiation.
    b. convection.
    c. conduction.
    d. absorption.

3. Substances that are poor conductors of heat (wood, plastic) are called

    a. insulators.
    b. radiators.
    c. resistors.
    d. amplifiers.

4. Energy of an object in motion is called

    a. potential energy.
    b. momentum energy.
    c. kinetic energy.
    d. heat capacity.

5. The process of heat energy moving through empty space is called

   a. radiation.
   b. convection.
   c. conduction.
   d. adsorption.

6. A large rock resting on a hill is an example of

   a. potential energy.
   b. kinetic energy.
   c. radiation energy.
   d. absorption energy.

7. Heat energy traveling from the sun to the earth is an example of

   a. radiation.
   b. convection.
   c. conduction.
   d. absorption.

8. The amount of heat gained or lost by a substance is commonly measured in

   a. meters.
   b. grams.
   c. liters.
   d. calories.

9. When fuel is consumed, most of the energy is changed into

   a. light.
   b. heat.
   c. movement.
   d. water.

10. The law of conservation of energy states that

    a. energy can be created but not destroyed.
    b. energy cannot be created but can be destroyed.
    c. energy can neither be created nor destroyed.
    d. energy can be created and destroyed.

Content Cluster: ENERGY IN THE EARTH SYSTEM

Objective: To evaluate knowledge of how actions on the Earth's surface are affected by radiation and convection currents.

> **Parent Tip:** The solar energy (from the sun) is the major energy that powers winds, ocean currents, and the water cycle. Heat reaches the earth's surface through convection and solar energy through radiation. Heat energy is distributed into the atmosphere and the oceans.

1. The movement of hot air from the Earth's surface out into the atmosphere because of temperature differences is an example of

    a. conduction currents.
    b. radiation currents.
    c. convection currents.
    d. electrical currents.

2. Convection currents in the ocean would move water

    a. from the warm surface down to the cooler depths.
    b. from a cooler area up to the warmer surface.
    c. from a cool area into an area of a hot thermal vent.
    d. all of the above

3. When water is changed from a liquid to a gas by the heat energy from the sun, it is called

    a. condensation.
    b. evaporation.
    c. transpiration.
    d. precipitation.

4. Visible light that reaches the Earth from the sun is also known as

    a. ultraviolet light.
    b. infrared light.
    c. solar light.
    d. white light.

5. When an object appears green in color, this is because

    a. green light is absorbed by the object.
    b. green light is reflected by the object.
    c. blue and yellow light are being absorbed by the object.
    d. blue and yellow light are being reflected by the object.

Content Cluster: ECOLOGY

Objective: To evaluate knowledge about the way organisms exchange energy and nutrients among themselves and with the environment.

Parent Tip: Ecology is the study of the interrelationships of plants, animals and the environment. The term *ecosystem* refers to the interacting system of living things in their non-living surroundings. Energy entering an ecosystem as sunlight is first changed into chemical energy by producers. This energy is passed from organism in food webs by animals eating plants and other animals.

Choose the correct answer.

1. Another name for a producer is a(n)

    a. autotroph.
    b. heterotroph.
    c. carnivore.
    d. parasite.

2. The process by which green plants take energy from the sun to make their own food is called

    a. respiration.
    b. digestion.
    c. photosynthesis.
    d. propagation.

3. A distinct level of feeding in an ecosystem (producer, consumer, decomposer, etc) is called a

    a. food web.
    b. energy pyramid.
    c. symbiosis.
    d. trophic level.

4. The sequence of one organism from one trophic level feeding upon another from a lower trophic level is called a

    a. parasitism.
    b. food chain.
    c. biocycle.
    d. population.

5. Food webs are interconnected food chains. As energy is passed from one trophic level to the next, which of the following happens?

    a. The available energy for the organisms remains the same.
    b. The available energy for the organisms increase.
    c. The available energy for the organisms is much less (less than 10% of the level above).
    d. The available energy for the organisms is sometimes greater and sometimes smaller than the level above.

6. In a food web all organisms but those in the first trophic level are

    a. carnivores.
    b. herbivores.
    c. autotrophs.
    d. heterotrophs.

7. All of the following organisms are producers except

    a. plants.
    b. sea weed.
    c. plankton.
    d. fish.

8. What is the difference between abiotic and biotic factor in an ecosystem?

    a. Biotic factors are living organisms while abiotic factors are non living parts of of the environment.
    b. Abiotic factors are found in aquatic ecosystems while biotic factors are found in terrestrial ecosystems.
    c. Biotic factors were formed when the earth was forming; abiotic factors have been formed recently.
    d. Biotic factors are non-living parts of the environment while abiotic factors are living organisms.

9. First order consumers eat what material?

    a. herbivores
    b. carnivores
    c. plants
    d. fungus

10. What do the nitrogen cycle, water cycle, and carbon cycle all have in common?

    a. They all disappeared along with the dinosaurs.
    b. All of the compounds are recycled through the decomposition of dead organisms.
    c. None of these materials are found in the atmosphere.
    d. All of these materials are lost at the end of each cycle.

11. What do second order consumers feed upon?

    a. plants
    b. herbivores
    c. carnivores
    d. fungus

12. What is the function of decomposers such as bacteria and fungi in the ecosystem?

    a. to convert sunlight to chemical energy
    b. to break down and decay dead organisms
    c. to pass energy from a producer to a consumer
    d. to pass energy from a herbivore to a carnivore

13. Which of the following would be an abiotic factor in an ecosystem?

    a. light
    b. water
    c. wind
    d. all of the above

Content Clusters: RESOURCES

Objective: To evaluate knowledge about sources of energy, their distribution, and their usefulness in our environment.

> **Parent Tip**: Energy sources are considered renewable or nonrenewable. A natural resource that is recycled or replaced by natural processes is called a renewable resource. One that is available in limited amounts and is not replaced or recycled is a non-renewable resource. Our most important sources of energy are fossil fuels. These are the remains of organisms buried millions of years ago. The burning of fossil fuel to release the energy can cause air pollution.

1. Which of the following are renewable resources?

    a. Air.
    b. Water.
    c. Wild life.
    d. All of the above.

2. The burning of fossil fuels can cause all of the following EXCEPT

    a. smog
    b. acid rain
    c. greenhouse effect
    d. destruction of the ozone layer

3. An example of a fossil fuel is

    a. wood from trees
    b. coal or oil
    c. water
    d. solar energy

4. The greenhouse effect may result in all of the following EXCEPT

    a. global warming
    b. melting of the ice cap
    c. the permanent loss of significant numbers of animal and plant species
    d. better types of plants for food

SCIENCE ANSWER KEY

Plate Tectonics
1. a
2. d
3. c
4. d
5. b
6. c
7. a
8. b
9. b
10. b
11. a
12. c
13. b
14. d
15. a

Earth's Surface
1. a
2. d
3. d
4. b
5. c
6. b
7. b
8. b
9. d
10. a
11. c

Thermal Energy
1. c
2. b
3. a

4. c
5. a
6. a
7. a
8. d
9. b
10. c

Earth System
1. c
2. a
3. b
4. d
5. b

Ecology
1. a
2. c
3. d
4. b
5. c
6. d
7. d
8. a
9. c
10. b
11. b
12. b
13. d

Resources
1. d
2. d
3. b
4. d

NOTES